PARADISO

The Illuminations to Dante's Divine Comedy
by Giovanni di Paolo

PARADISO

The Illuminations to Dante's Divine Comedy by

GIOVANNI DI PAOLO

JOHN POPE-HENNESSY

RANDOM HOUSE

NEW YORK

Library of Congress Cataloging-in-Publication Data

Pope-Hennessy, John Wyndham, Sir
        Paradiso : the illuminations to Dante's Divine comedy by Giovanni
di Paolo / John Pope-Hennessy.
            p.   cm.
        ISBN 0-679-42821-6
        1. Giovanni, di Paolo, ca. 1403–ca. 1482—Criticism and
interpretation.   2. Dante Alighieri, 1265–1321.   Paradiso—
illustrations.   3. British Library.   Manuscript.   Yates-Thompson
36—illustrations.   4. Illumination of books and manuscripts.
Renaissance—Italy—Siena.   I. Giovanni, di Paolo, ca. 1403–ca.
1482.   II. Title.
ND3162.G57P67   1993
745.6'7'092—dc20   93-16598

                                                                        r93

MANUFACTURED IN JAPAN

24689753

First U.S. Edition

CONTENTS

To Jayne Wrightsman
friend
and bibliophile

This book is about the greatest of all poems. The third of the three sections or Cantiche of the *Divine Comedy*, the *Paradiso*, was composed in the years immediately preceding Dante's death in 1321. Less popular and less self-explanatory than its two predecessors, the *Inferno* and the *Purgatorio*, it is more highly personal in that it describes the intellectual and emotional responses of an individual to the experience of a journey through the celestial sphere. Its language and its use of metaphor and simile are incomparably rich, and it is filled with visual observations with which we, over six hundred years after its composition, can still identify.

Not unnaturally, the *Divine Comedy* was widely illustrated. The earliest narrative codices were produced in Florence in the fourth decade of the fourteenth century. One of them, by a Florentine pupil of the painter and miniaturist Pacino da Bonaguida, in the Biblioteca Laurenziana in Florence (Laur. Strozz. 152), appears to date from about 1335, and another, in Milan (Bib. Trivulziana Ms. 1080), illuminated by the Florentine miniaturist known as the Master of the Dominican Effigies, is dated in the year of Giotto's death, 1337. From then on a large number of illustrated manuscripts were produced. They were made in the main in the shops of professional illuminators, generally in the form of drawings in the margins or across the bottom of the page. Typical of the way in which they were conceived is a Venetian manuscript of 1345 at Budapest; it has small rectangular scenes illustrating the *Inferno* and part of the *Purgatorio*, but at Canto XII of the *Purgatorio* the illuminator suddenly stopped work, leaving in the manuscript five preliminary sanguine drawings whose subjects are indicated in writing underneath. Occasionally these Trecento illustrations to the *Divine Comedy* are substantial works of art – the most distinguished are two scenes from the *Inferno* at Perugia painted in Siena about 1340, possibly by Pietro Lorenzetti – but as a whole their interest lies in what they tell us about the way in which a reader visualised Dante's text at the time when they were made. With the fifteenth century, however, the illustrations to the Cantiche become more sophisticated. A manuscript in Paris by the Florentine illuminator Bartolomeo di Fruosino treats the episodes of the *Inferno* in terms of qualified life-likeness, and in Milan a miniaturist known as the Master of the Vitae Imperatorum depicts more explicitly than any of his predecessors not only the punishments of the damned, but the responses of Dante and Virgil to what they see. It is with this class of manuscript that the illuminations to the *Paradiso* illustrated in the present book belong.

1
2
4
3

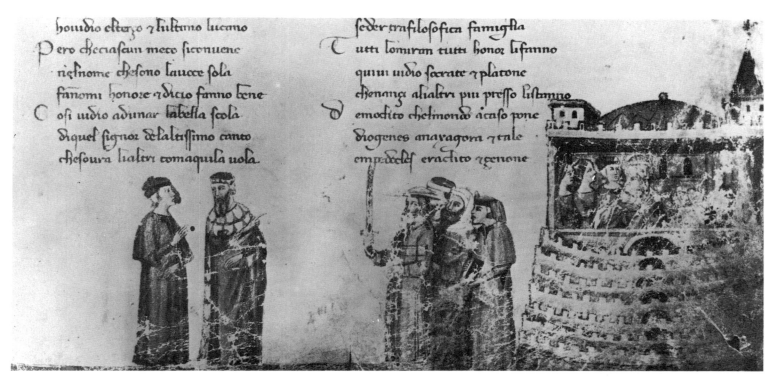

1. Florentine, c. 1335: *Dante and Virgil greeted by Homer, Horace, Ovid and Lucan, Inferno IV* (Biblioteca Laurenziana, Florence).

2. Venetian, c. 1345, preliminary drawing for *Dante and Virgil observe the wrathful, Purgatorio XVI* (University Library, Budapest).

3. Master of the Vitae Imperatorum:
*Dante and Virgil before Cerberus, Inferno
VI* (Bibliothèque Nationale, Paris).

4. Bartolomoeo di Fruosino, c. 1420:
*Dante and Virgil watch a devil striking the
sowers of discord, Inferno XXVIII*
(Bibliothèque Nationale, Paris).

5, 6. Pisanello: obverse and reverse of a medal of King Alfonso V of Aragon, 1449. (National Gallery of Art, Washington, D.C., Samuel H. Kress Collection).

Known as the Yates-Thompson Codex, after the name of the donor who bequeathed it to the British Library, it consists of one hundred and ninety leaves and contains one hundred and fifteen illuminations. Its pages measure fourteen and a half by ten inches. The text is written in a single column on the extreme left of each page (no doubt in order to leave room for annotation). Each Cantica is preceded by an historiated capital, each Canto by an elaborate floriated capital and each tercet by a small coloured initial on a golden ground. With the exception of its three historiated capitals, the illustrations take the form of oblong miniatures, which are of uniform height (the average height of the scenes in the *Inferno* and *Purgatorio* is 8.5cm., while those in the *Paradiso* average 9cm.) but varying width, wider in the case of scenes that are exceptionally complex, narrow in those with fewer figures. Set horizontally across the bottom of the page, they have heavy illusionistic frames, sometimes attached with fictive stitching to the parchment, sometimes composed of strap work, and sometimes decorated with a punch. As a result the miniatures assume a coherence and consistency far greater than that of scenes in any earlier Dante manuscript. As we turn the pages of the book, the effect is that of a sequence of images on a television screen.

The Codex was illuminated, and is likely also to have been written, in Siena, and its exceptional quality is due to the patron for whom it was prepared. On the first page it bears the arms of Aragon, and it must therefore have been commissioned by, or designed for presentation to, Alfonso V of Aragon, King of Naples, the creator of the Biblioteca Alfonsina, one of the great humanist libraries. The nucleus of the library had been formed in Spain, and inventories of it made at Barcelona in 1412 and at Valencia in 1417 show that

p.37

5,6

initially it consisted in the main of French and Spanish manuscripts. In 1432 it was transferred to Italy, and thereafter it expanded rapidly with the acquisition of Italian, Latin and Greek codices. The principal librarian was invariably Spanish, but in the 1430s it owed its growth to the advice of Italian humanists, among them Guiniforte Barzizza, Lorenzo Valla, Panormita and Beccadelli. For Alfonso manuscripts were treasure trove, and there are repeated references in the royal account books to the purchase of classical texts – a Seneca acquired in Milan, three books from the library of Petrarch purchased in Genoa, texts of Claudian and Silius Italicus secured in Venice, and Florentine manuscripts bought on the advice of Vespasiano da Bisticci. The library remained in Naples until, in 1538, it was transferred to Spain, where it was housed in the monastery of San Miguel de los Reyes at Valencia. A catalogue made of it there lists five Dante manuscripts. One of these, of which a fuller account is given in a later inventory, is probably identical with the present manuscript. The provenance of the codex from Valencia is confirmed by a partly illegible inscription on the first page.

The association of Siena on the one hand and Alfonso of Aragon on the other may at first sight seem a strange one. It resulted from ambition and topography. Unlike Florence, which successfully resisted the forces of the Dukes of Milan at the very beginning of the fifteenth century and again during the 1420s, Siena and the contado on which its wealth was based were isolated and were not readily defensible. The city therefore tended for pragmatic reasons to ally itself either with Naples or with Milan. In 1399 Giovanni Galeazzo Visconti, whose forces at the time were fighting against Florence, was invested with the lordship of Siena. The alliance proved less onerous than it might have been, since within three years the Duke of Milan died. But the Sienese were constitutionally anti-Florentine, and after four short years of peace the city entered into an anti-Florentine alliance with King Ladislaus of Naples. By 1416, however, the Angevin dynasty in Naples was under pressure from a young claimant to the throne, Alfonso of Aragon, operating from Palermo. Naples and indeed the whole of Southern Italy were in a state of civil war, and only in 1442 was the situation finally resolved when the city of Naples surrendered to Alfonso. Through the middle of the fifteenth century the Aragonese kingdom of Naples, covering Sardinia and Sicily and an area from Reggio to the Abruzzi, was the largest state in Italy. But Alfonso's aims were more ambitious. His objective was a Mediterranean empire based on Naples and Aragon, and though he desisted from attacking Rome, military operations spread to western Tuscany.

Florence supported the Angevin claimant to the throne of Naples, but Siena, to the King's annoyance, adopted a position of neutrality. Siena, Alfonso declared, was like the first storey of a house, defiled by urine dripping from the floor above and by smoke from the kitchen beneath. None the less he respected Sienese neutrality. For Siena, exposed as it would otherwise have been to Neapolitan control, the only permissible policy was appeasement. When the occupation of Monte Argentario brought the threat of war dangerously close, the event was celebrated in Siena with a bonfire, the straw for which was supplied by a Sienese member of the King's entourage, Antonio Morosini, and in June 1442 Alfonso's capture of Naples was also celebrated publicly. A Sienese, Lodovico di Salimbene Petroni, was knighted at this time by Alfonso, and later, during the war on Sienese territory, served as ambassador to the Neapolitan army. In October 1447 two delegates from Siena, Ghino Bellanti and Jacomo di Guiduccio, were despatched to Alfonso's headquarters 'con un bello e ricco presente' in the company of several hundred Sienese boys who were anxious to see the Neapolitan camp. A number of miniatures in the Yates-Thompson codex contain armorial details or interpolated scenes flattering to Alfonso. The evidence of the miniatures is that the manuscript was illuminated in the middle of the 1440s, and a possible date for the commission is the spring of 1444, when a peace conference was summoned by Pope Eugenius IV to meet in Siena. There is, however, no means of telling whether the Codex was commissioned by Alfonso in Siena or was ordered for presentation to Alfonso by some intermediary.

One of its peculiarities is that the miniatures in it were executed by two different artists. The first was responsible for illustrating the *Inferno* and the *Purgatorio* and the second for the *Paradiso*. The initial letter of the first page of the *Paradiso* is, however, by the first artist not the second, and the three final Cantos of the *Purgatorio* (XXX, XXXI, XXXII), in which the figure of Beatrice, the protagonist of the *Paradiso*, should properly make her first appearance, are not illustrated. Evidently there was some change of plan. Either the Codex was abandoned by the first artist and then taken over by the second, or the two artists worked concurrently to ensure speedy completion of the book.

The *Divine Comedy* is a difficult poem and even in the fourteenth century needed exposition if the thought embodied in it was to be fully understood. For this reason there sprang up an academic Dante literature which took the form of commentaries added as marginal notes to Dante's text. In some cases the names of the commentators are recorded – they include Jacopo della Lana, the author of a commentary written at Bologna in 1324; Dante's son Pietro Alighieri, whose commentary was written between 1340 and 1358; Guido da Pisa; Francesco Buti; Boccaccio (on the *Inferno* only); and Benvenuto da Imola – but many of the commentaries are anonymous. One of them, the most highly regarded commentary of all, is the *Ottimo Commento*. The earliest Florentine commentary, it is dateable to 1333–1334, and its author has been conjecturally identified as Ser Andrea di Ser Lancia. It is, as its title suggests, the most lucid and most serviceable of the commentaries. Its aim was to 'sponere le oscurità che sono in questo libro intitulato Commedie', and it is successful in doing this. It is learned – a note on the concept of Justice presented by Dante in Canto XVIII of the *Paradiso* contains textual references to Cicero, Seneca, Macrobius,

Isidore of Seville and St Augustine – but seldom is it so elaborate as to occlude the text. A number of the miniatures in the Yates-Thompson Codex illustrate historical and other scenes that are not described by Dante, and these have their source in the *Ottimo Commento*.

It would be wrong, however, to suppose that the illuminations were the outcome of a one-to-one relationship between the artists involved and an annotated copy of the poem. At universities the *Divine Comedy* was the subject of close study, and it was widely read in public. In Florence in the fifteenth century its most popular expositor was Frate Antonio da Arezzo, who lectured on it in the Duomo, and in Siena a member of the University faculty, Giovanni di ser Buccio da Spoleto, was under contract to read, on feast days, outside the church of San Vigilio, 'il libro di Dante.' Born about 1370, Giovanni di ser Buccio joined the staff of the university in Siena in 1396 as a teacher of grammar and rhetoric, was still employed there in 1432–1433, and was reconfirmed in 1442. Soon after, he was dismissed on grounds of age, but in 1445 he was still receiving a pension of thirty florins a year. He was well thought of as an instructor, and numbered among his pupils the future San Bernardino and, in 1423, the future Pope Pius II. The two artists of the present codex would certainly have heard him declaiming Dante, and he or some other member of the university staff may well have acted as consultant on their work.

Within a few years of Dante's death the *Inferno* and *Purgatorio* had a deep influence on monumental fresco painting. The punishments described in them, when translated from literary into visual terms, put a premium on the depiction of active naked figures subjected to the torments Dante described. The first artist who responded to this challenge was Orcagna in a great fresco of the Last Judgment in Santa Croce, in which the nude is handled, evidently on the basis of life study, with astonishing vigour and resource. Nowhere in book illumination is there an equivalent for this great work. Through the middle of the fourteenth century the nudes in Dante codices are cartoon-like figures lacking in physical authority. Early in the fifteenth century their style becomes more confident and more inventive, as in a Dante illumination by Bartolomeo di Fruosino and his assistants in Paris (Bib. Nat. it. 74) 7 which includes a miniature of the topography of Hell based on the formidable fresco by Nardo di Cione in Santa Maria Novella. The rendering of the human figure, however, remains so insecure that the Carnal Sinners in Canto V of the *Inferno* float like dirigibles across the scene. The author of the illuminations to the *Inferno* and *Purgatorio* in the Yates-Thompson Codex was an artist of a different stamp. His scenes in the *Inferno* take place on a 8 rock-strewn stage, from which the eye is carried back to craggy mountains sometimes represented at a distance and sometimes pressing into the foreground space. The mountains are invariably lit from the left, and are so constructed that they establish a continuum of movement from left to right. Never is their form or the alternating patches of light and shadow with which they are constructed exactly reproduced. It has been suggested that the

7. Bartolomeo di Fruosino c. 1420: *Dante and Virgil observe Minos judging the souls of carnal sinners*, *Inferno V* (Bibliothèque Nationale, Paris).

8. Vecchietta: *Dante addressing Guido da Montefeltro*, *Inferno XXVII* (British Library, London).

artist of this part of the Codex 'turned back to an older model that must have had illustrations in a continuous frieze', but the disposition of the figures in the individual scenes renders this most improbable. Like the mountains in the background, the naked occupants of Hell are lit strongly from the left. Typical of them is the profile figure of Guido da Montefeltro (Canto XXVII) whose back, in shadow, is drawn with a dark outline but whose face and body are strongly lit. This procedure recalls that of Domenico Veneziano in the *Adoration of the Magi* in Berlin and the *Young Baptist in the Wilderness* in Washington where the figures are lit, more subtly, from one side. In the scene of Dante and Virgil rowed by Phlegyas across the river Styx (Canto VIII), the treatment of the swimmers is masterly. Illustrators of the *Inferno* were required, however, to describe not only punishment of the Damned, but Dante's reaction to them, and throughout the scenes his horror and Virgil's reassurance are treated with great sensibility.

By whom were the *Inferno* and *Purgatorio* illustrated? When I first discussed them, half a century ago, I concluded that they were the work of the Sienese painter Vecchietta. In 1964 this ascription was rejected by Meiss, who gave them instead to a minor Sienese artist,

8

10

9. Vecchietta: *Three Circles of the Violent, Inferno XI* (British Library, London).

10. Vecchietta: *Dante and Virgil crossing the Styx, Inferno VIII* (British Library, London).

11. Vecchietta: *Last Judgment*, fresco (Baptistry of Siena Cathedral).

Priamo della Quercia, and later republished them under the same name. I believe this view to be wrong on the simple ground that attributions must be based upon similitude and that the miniatures bear no resemblance to Priamo della Quercia's scanty authenticated works. At the same time, I felt sceptical of my own theory. But our knowledge of Vecchietta has since been extended by the cleaning of the frescoes of the Baptistry in Siena, on which he was

11 at work in 1450. In the *Last Judgment* on the ceiling of the Baptistry the running figures in the background conform exactly to those in the illuminations, while in the adjacent fresco of the

12 *Christ in Limbo* the figures that reach out from the cavern assume positions that recur in the

9 *Three Circles of the Violent* (f. 20r.) and the *Punishment of the Traitors in the Frozen Marsh* (f. 59r.). Vecchietta's authorship of the illuminations to the *Inferno* and the *Purgatorio* now seems to me self-evident.

12. Vecchietta: *Christ in Limbo*, fresco (Baptistry of Siena Cathedral).

The *Paradiso* by its very nature was more resistant to illustration than the other Cantiche and was indeed less often illustrated. Whereas the episodes in the *Inferno* and *Purgatorio* are concrete and strongly visual, the encounters in the *Paradiso* are veiled in mystery. A nineteenth century commentator describes its subject in terms that explain the insuperable difficulty of providing a pictorial equivalent for Dante's text:

> To understand Dante's conception of Paradise, we must imagine the universe as consisting of nine spheres concentric with the earth, which is fixed at the centre, and surrounded by the spheres of air and fire. The sphere of fire is immediately in contact with that of the Moon, beyond which come in order those of Mercury, Venus, the Sun, Mars, Jupiter, Saturn, and the fixed stars. The last of all is the sphere of the First Movement, or Primum Mobile, which governs the general motion of the heavens from east

to west, and by which all place and time is ultimately measured. Each of these is under the direction of one of the angelic orders, and exercises its special influence on earthly affairs. The three lowest spheres are allotted to the souls of those whose life on earth was marred by yielding to the temptations of the world; the next four to those whose actions were wholly directed by virtuous motives. The last two have no special tenants assigned to them, but appear to serve as common places of meeting, the one to saints, the other to angels. Finally, outside of all, comes the Empyrean heaven, where is neither time nor place but light only; the special abode of Deity and resting place of the saints.

The range of options offered by the text was very large. To take one instance only, the celebrated scene in which Dante is interrogated by St Peter (Canto XXIV) was represented 14   in the fourteenth century with Dante, accompanied by Beatrice, standing or kneeling before a full-length figure of the Saint. But the *Paradiso* does not describe the physical presence of St Peter. He is 'un foco' and is addressed by Beatrice as 'eternal light of the great man with whom Our Lord left the keys,' a 'blessed flame' from which there issued the injunction recorded in the poem. When Botticelli, at the end of the fifteenth century, prepared his 13   drawings for the *Divine Comedy*, he showed this scene as Dante describes it, with radiating circles of small flames, beneath one of which is the word 'piero'. Before work on the Yates-Thompson Codex started two firm decisions seem to have been made. In most earlier illustrated manuscripts the protagonists, Dante and Beatrice, stand on the ground and the planets and their occupants are shown in the sky. But in the present Codex the two main figures, and the spirits by whom they are addressed, occupy celestial space, while the stories that they tell are represented on the ground. In Siena there was a long tradition of scenes in which celestial intervention played some part, and the figures of Dante and Beatrice are shown in flight, like the figures of the Saint in Simone Martini's Beato Agostino Novello altarpiece, with the same linearity and the same attribute of weightlessness. As a result the scenes, with their delicate blue skies and dark blue backgrounds, transmit more clearly than any earlier Dante illustrations a sense of other worldliness. It was, moreover, decided that the spheres and planets should be represented not as the simple circles that were usual in the fourteenth century, but with a radiance and colour that would, in some fashion, reflect the emphasis on light and colour in the poem; and that one and all should be parallel to the picture plane.

*   *   *

13. Botticelli: *Dante and Beatrice before St. Peter, Paradiso* XXIV (Staatliche Museen zu Berlin).

14. Italian mid-fourteenth century: *Dante and Beatrice before St. Peter, Paradiso* XXIV (Bibliothèque de l'Arsenal, Paris).

15. Giovanni di Paolo: *The Suffering and Triumphant Christ* (Pinacoteca Nazionale, Siena).

Luckily Giovanni di Paolo, who was entrusted with the *Paradiso*, was an artist of exceptional visionary quality. We know very little about his origins. His birthdate is not recorded; it is traditionally given as 1403, but was probably five or ten years earlier, and he was therefore a few years older than his Sienese contemporaries Sassetta and Sano di Pietro. His affinities from the beginning were with the Dominican convent of San Domenico, and his first recorded commission, in 1417, was for illuminating a book of hours paid for by the convent librarian. In Siena the prime devotional cult was that of a Dominican tertiary, Catherine of Siena, who had died in 1380 and whose *Legenda maior* was in course of compilation in the 1390s by her confessor Raymond of Capua. In 1418 a small panel of the as yet uncanonised Saint was ordered from Giovanni di Paolo on behalf of a nun in the convent of Santa Marta. One very early work, seemingly painted for the altar of Francesco Bellanti, Bishop of Grosseto, in San Domenico, survives, a panel of the *Suffering and*   15 *Triumphant Christ*, now in the Pinacoteca Nazionale in Siena. On the left stands the emaciated figure of the suffering Christ, holding the cross with preternaturally long fingers against his shoulder and with blood pouring from his feet. On the right, supported on the wings of trumpeting cherubim, sits Christ in judgement, with hand raised and blood draining from his side. Beneath, presided over by St Michael, are two caverns containing the blessed and the damned. Seldom in the Quattrocento in Siena did any painter affirm, so unambiguously and at so early a stage, the visionary course he was destined to pursue.

Siena, in the first two decades of the fifteenth century, was culturally isolated, but after 1416 a great Florentine sculptor, Ghiberti, paid spasmodic visits there, influencing both Sassetta (the architecture of whose early predella panels is profoundly Ghibertesque) and Giovanni di Paolo, whose small *St Jerome in his Study* in the Siena gallery, is also, in its delicate handling of space, redolent of Ghiberti. Of still greater consequence was the arrival, in the summer of 1425, of a major North Italian painter, Gentile da Fabriano. Born in the Marches, Gentile had worked with great success in Venice in the Palazzo Ducale and at Brescia in the Broletto, where his frescoes attracted the interest of the new Pope Martin V, who invited him to work in Rome. In September 1419 Gentile left Brescia to join the Pope in Florence, and there he painted two revolutionary altarpieces, the first, completed in May 1423, the celebrated *Adoration of the Magi* for the Strozzi Chapel in Santa Trinita, now in the   16 Uffizi, and the second the dispersed *Quaratesi Polyptych* completed in May 1425 for San   17 Niccolo. A month later, on his way to Rome, he visited Siena, where he painted a lost polyptych, the *Madonna de' Notai*. Work in Siena occupied him till September and was interrupted by the commission for a fresco in Orvieto Cathedral, after which he returned to Siena to complete the polyptych. By January 1427 he was at work in Rome, where in the late summer he died. Gentile was an important figure, and his life style was that of a person of consequence. When he left Brescia in 1419 he travelled with seven assistants and craftsmen,

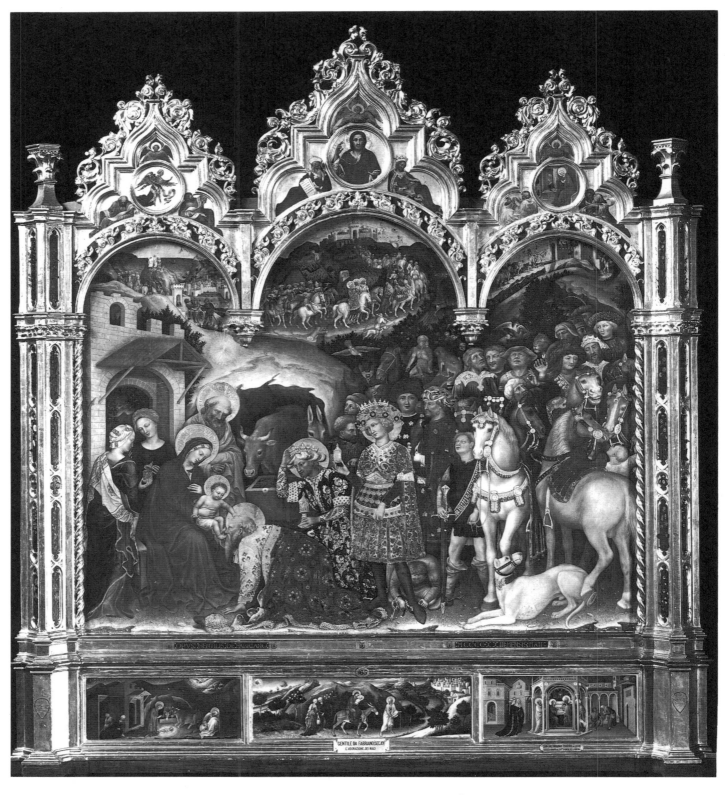

16. Gentile da Fabriano: *Adoration of the Magi* (Uffizi, Florence). The right hand predella panel is a copy of the original now in the Louvre (see ill. 28).

17. Gentile da Fabriano: *Madonna and Child*, from the Quaratesi Polyptych (Royal Collection).

18. Giovanni di Paolo: *Madonna enthroned with Angels* (Prepositura, Castelnuovo Berardenga).

and a retinue on the same scale must have accompanied him to Siena, hence the deep impression his arrival made. It was at one time supposed that Giovanni di Paolo worked with Gentile in Siena. Certainly the relations between them must, for a short time, have been very close, since Gentile's opulent technique was rapidly assimilated by the younger artist.

This is most evident in an altarpiece painted for the Malevolti chapel in San Domenico which carries the inscription OPUS JOHANNIS SENENSIS MCCCCXXVI. All that survives of its main panels are a *Madonna enthroned with Angels*, at Castelnuovo Berardenga, and two full length Saints, the Baptist and St Dominic, in the Pinacoteca Nazionale at Siena. The cartoon of the Virgin and Child recalls the altarpieces of the most popular Sienese painter of the first two decades of the century, Taddeo di Bartolo, but upon it is superimposed a richness and refinement peculiar to Gentile. This is especially evident in the suave line of the Virgin's cloak, in the acorns on her gilded dress, in the perspective crown held over her head, in the eight olive-wreathed angels, and in the alternating thistles and mount of Paradise on the tiled floor. Four of its surviving predella panels are at

18

19, 20. Giovanni di Paolo: *Raising of Lazarus* and *Deposition* (Walters Art Gallery, Baltimore).

19   Baltimore. One of them, the *Raising of Lazarus*, is based on the same scene from Duccio's *Maesta*, then on the high altar of the Duomo in Siena. But where Duccio's figures are sober and restrained, Giovanni di Paolo's are voluble and animated. An inquisitive head peers round the cover of the tomb, and the spectators are shown excitedly discussing the event. In

20   the *Deposition* two converging ladders, in front of and behind the Cross, manifest an interest in geometry that reappears in many of the artist's later paintings. The most vivid of the panels, the *Entombment*, like the full-length St John above, may derive from a Byzantine manuscript, but the strongly lit figure of Nicodemus at the back casting a menacing shadow on the wall again recalls Gentile.

      A year later, in 1427, Giovanni di Paolo painted yet another altarpiece for San

21   Domenico, this time for the Branchini altar. The central panel, in the Norton Simon collection at Pasadena, has two inscriptions; one on the frame gives the artist's name and the date of the painting, while the other, in the halo of the Virgin, is personal: 'HIC QUI TE PINXIT PROTEGE VIRGO VIRUM.' The frame of Duccio's high altar in Siena Cathedral carries a personal inscription: MATER SCA DEI/SIS CAUSA SENIS REQUIEI/SIS DUCCIO VITA/TE QUIA PINXIT ITA, but the prayer in the halo of the Branchini Madonna, in the form of a classical pentameter, is still more intimate. The Virgin is a Madonna of Humility represented as Queen of Heaven, wearing a gesso crown and a cloak lined with ermine, and is supported by four seraphim whose wings protrude beneath her dress. The seraphim continue above, three at each side, their wings outstretched against the golden ground. The ermine lining of the cloak falls with great elegance, and becomes visible once more at the bottom on the right and at a point on the left

21. Giovanni di Paolo: *Madonna and Child* (The Norton Simon Foundation, Pasadena).

22, 23. Floreated pilaster panels from Gentile da Fabriano's *Adoration of the Magi* (Uffizi, Florence; left) and Giovanni di Paolo's *St. John the Baptist entering the Wilderness* (National Gallery, London; right).

where the cloak is turned back on itself. The base of the painting is strewn with severed flowers. Whereas in the Madonna of the previous year the lessons to be learned from Gentile da Fabriano were applied to a conventional Sienese Madonna type, here integration is complete. The face of the Virgin is rounder and less austere. One of the most beautiful features is the Child reaching up to touch the Virgin's throat. There is no precedent for this moving figure in Sienese painting, but it has parallels in Florence in the work of Masolino.

Giovanni di Paolo responded to Gentile's fascination with the natural world. In

22   Gentile's *Adoration of the Magi* in the Uffizi the pilasters are filled not, as was customary, with standing saints, but with sprigs of flowering plants, among them camomile, broom, chicory, crocus, and morning glory, adapted from a pattern book that showed them in different stages of development. In Giovanni di Paolo's Branchini Madonna similar sprigs of flowers — white roses depicted from four different views, cornflowers and marigolds — cover the

23   ground. Similar flowers occur in many of his later paintings. They intrude into the interstices of a predella in the middle of the 1430s, and in some of the paintings produced at the extreme end of his life, roses, by this time rather arthritic roses, are found once more.

After 1427, Gentile remained for Giovanni di Paolo a living force. In a triptych painted about 1432 for the parish church at Baschi, near Orvieto, the figures, with their dense facture and their gilt gesso ornament, are still Gentilesque. They remain so in a major altarpiece painted in 1436 for the Fondi chapel in the church of San Francesco in Siena. The church of San Francesco was gravely damaged by fire in 1655, and among the casualties was Giovanni di Paolo's painting. The centre and left hand panels were badly burned and the

24   *Madonna and Child* was cut down to half-length and inserted in a street tabernacle. Its style is more fluid than that of the Branchini Madonna, but the features once more reflect Gentile, and the Child, lying across the Virgin's lap with right arm extended to the onlooker, is adapted from the central panel of Gentile's Quaratesi altarpiece in Florence.

Religious life in Tuscany in the second quarter of the fifteenth century was dominated by two reforming movements, the Franciscan Observance, which had as its protagonist San Bernardino and as its epicentre the Convent of the Osservanza outside Siena, and the Dominican Observance, established first at Fiesole and then in Florence at San Marco. Especially influential in Siena were the cycles of sermons that San Bernardino preached in 1427 in the Piazza del Campo, in 1434 in the Piazza San Francesco, and to the Disciplinati della Scala in the Spedale della Scala. Their tenor was mystical, but it was mysticism adapted to the practical needs of daily life, and may well have stimulated the uncompromisingly literal quality of Giovanni di Paolo's imagination. The only surviving

25   picture he painted for the Osservanza is a large *Crucifixion* now in the Pinacoteca at Siena, inscribed HOC OPUS JOHANNES PAULI DE SENIS PINXIT MCCCCXXXX. The height of the panel is used to give maximum strength to the body

24. Giovanni di Paolo: *Madonna and Child*
(Monte dei Paschi di Siena).

25. Giovanni di Paolo: *Crucifixion* (Pinacoteca
Nazionale, Siena).

of Christ, and the Cross is extended at the top with the label INRI and a nesting pelican. The Gothic moulding of the frame severs the fingers of Christ's bleeding hands. The depth of the Cross is established by heavy shadows beneath its arms and the body of Christ, with a transparent perizoma, is lit from the left. Beneath the Cross in profile is the red-clad Magdalen holding Christ's legs, and the Virgin and St John, one a closed silhouette and the other moving forwards with arms raised. Apart from a lost panel formerly in Vienna and a painted Cross in Dublin this is the only large-scale Crucifixion by Giovanni di Paolo that we know, but elements adapted from it were employed in a number of smaller panels, and continued in use till the penultimate decade of the painter's life.

Most of Giovanni di Paolo's predellas have been broken up and his development as a narrative artist is for that reason less easy to trace. The predella of the altarpiece of 1426 is followed by a second Passion predella, of which one panel is at Philadelphia and two are in the Vatican. In the *Deposition* one of the ladders leaning against the Cross in the painting at Baltimore is retained, the body of Christ has the same tension and three of the other figures are wrapped in the same tightly folded robes. The only direct points of association with Gentile are a gesso sun pouring its light on the *Deposition* from the left and the cartoons of St Peter and another apostle in the *Agony in the Garden*. Possibly Giovanni di Paolo's scenes come from the predella of the Branchini altarpiece of 1427. There follow, about 1435, three parts of a disassembled predella in the Siena gallery, a *Presentation of the Virgin in the Temple*, a *Crucifixion*, and a *Flight into Egypt*. The latter is Giovanni di Paolo's first great landscape painting. The principal figures are spaced out across the foreground. Behind them is a row of trees, beyond which is a peasant hut lit from the top left corner by a gesso sun casting a shadow forwards on two peasants trenching the ground. Behind the hut, on a lower level, runs a river with a lock or mill on its further bank, and beyond this again are two labourers, one of them ploughing, some trees which again cast their shadows forward, and a small town set on a rising rock and backed by distant hills. The blue of the sky deepens as it approaches the upper edge of the small panel and across it there fly four cranes.

It appears (and the evidence for this is wholly visual) that about 1440 Giovanni di Paolo saw the works of Fra Angelico and Gentile da Fabriano in Florence in the original. The reason for supposing this is that four out of five scenes in a predella painted about this time depend from originals in Florence. Alternatively drawings from them were made in Florence for his use. In either case their employment would have been due to the commissioning body. The institution in Siena with the closest Florentine contacts was the Spedale della Scala, from which Giovanni di Paolo received a commission in 1440 for an altarpiece for the chapel of the infirmary hospital adjacent to one of the women's wards. The significant aspect of these little paintings is, however, dissimilarity not likeness. In the *Annunciation* the central group depends from Fra Angelico, though the architecture of the

26

26. Giovanni di Paolo: *Flight into Egypt* (Pinacoteca Nazionale, Siena).

27. Giovanni di Paolo: *Presentation in the Temple* (The Metropolitan Museum of Art, New York, Gift of George Blumenthal, 1941).

28. Gentile da Fabriano: *Presentation in the Temple* (Louvre, Paris), predella panel from the Uffizi *Adoration* (see ill. 16).

setting is very different. Gentile da Fabriano's horizontal *Nativity* is replanned as an upright composition, and the *Annunciation to the Shepherds* takes place in a circular burst of light with the shepherds standing, not seated on the ground. With the *Adoration of the Magi* similar changes occur; the composition is abbreviated on the right and the distant procession of the Magi is omitted. The *Presentation in the Temple* is likewise compressed with a new emphasis   27
on verticality. A high viewing point replaces the low viewing point adopted by Gentile and   28
we look down on the temple floor. The upper part of the temple reads like a Northern miniature by Broederlam. Two figurative changes are also made. A priest is inserted centrally behind the altar (the reason for this is that a priest appears behind the altar in a canonical Sienese trecento painting of the scene by Ambrogio Lorenzetti), and in the lower right hand corner, marked by displaced marble slabs, is a hole in the ground. Described in these terms, Giovanni di Paolo's panel may sound derivative, but it reads as an original creation, and it does so because the idiom into which the composition was translated was, for Siena, progressive and highly personal.

Another Dominican altarpiece, for the Guelfi chapel in San Domenico, is dated 1445. Now in the Uffizi, its five main panels show the Virgin and Child flanked by Saints Peter   29
and Paul and two Dominican saints, Dominic and Thomas Aquinas. The Virgin is seated, supported by seraphim whose wings extend up the side of the panel. Her seat or throne is covered by an extension of her dress whose rippling folds fall on the ground. The

altarpiece is described in the middle of the seventeenth century in a source which records beneath the main panels a predella showing 'il giudizio finale, il diluvio e la creazione del mondo (cose bellissime).' The panel of the Flood has disappeared, but there survive, in the Metropolitan Museum of Art, the scene of the Creation of the World (which stood under the St Dominic) and a Paradise which abutted on the left side of the Last Judgment. Paradise is a meadow filled with flowers, backed by a line of trees with golden fruit, whose trunks are outlined against a blue sky that pales as it reaches the horizon. The figures in it are shown greeting one another. In the centre St Monica greets St Augustine, to the left an angel welcomes the Beato Ambrogio Sansedoni, below two Dominicans embrace, and to their right a hermit is shown in conversation with two nuns. Whereas in Fra Angelico's *Last*

29. Giovanni di Paolo: *Madonna and Child with Saints* (Uffizi, Florence).

30. Giovanni di Paolo: *Creation and Expulsion from Paradise* (The Metropolitan Museum of Art, New York, Robert Lehman Collection, 1975).

Judgment in the Museo di San Marco the blessed are shown adoring Christ, here they are presented as guests at some idyllic garden party. In the upper right-hand corner an angel, lit with celestial radiance and facing to the right, leads a diffident young man towards the missing central scene. The scene is cut on the right, but must have continued with a central Christ in Judgment and on its right the damned consigned to Hell.

    Adjacent to this panel at the left end of the predella stood the inspired scene of the *Creation of the World and the Expulsion from Paradise*. In the *Expulsion*, which fills a little less than half the panel, Paradise is once more represented as a garden filled with flowers and shaded by seven trees, but on this occasion the four rivers of Paradise are included at the bottom of the scene. The naked figures of Eve, Adam and the Archangel form a frieze across the middle ground, in poses adapted from a work any Sienese would recognise, the relief of

30

the Expulsion carved by Jacopo della Quercia for the Fonte Gaia in the Campo. From the upper left corner God the Father, in a blue robe supported by blue cherubim and surrounded by a gold and yellow aureole, plunges down with his right hand extended to set in motion a large zodiacal sphere. The sphere contains in the centre a *mappamondo* or plan of the known earth surrounded by the zones of water, air and fire, and the circles of the seven planets. Beyond these is the band of the zodiac and beyond this again is the blue band of the *primum mobile*. In Siena this beautifully rendered image would have struck a responsive chord. In a room in the Palazzo Pubblico still known as the Sala del Mappamondo, Ambrogio Lorenzetti, a hundred years before, had painted what Ghiberti describes as 'a Cosmography, that is a representation of all the habitable earth,' and an earlier zodiacal fresco has since been discovered on one wall at the end of the same room. These are the monumental progenitors of the brilliant illuminations to the *Paradiso* in the Yates-Thompson Codex. The connection of the illuminations with the imagery and style of Giovanni di Paolo's predella panel of the *Creation of the World* is indeed so intimate, both on a narrative and a decorative plane, as to leave little doubt that the miniatures date from about this time, and were probably executed about 1445.

This stylistic inference is buttressed by the fact that two miniatures (f. 145r. and f. 159r.) contain views of Florence dominated by the Duomo. In both cases the Duomo is depicted after the completion of Brunelleschi's cupola but without the central lantern and the exedras built by Brunelleschi over the transepts at the east end of the church. The two miniatures (or the drawings from which they probably depend) are likely, therefore, to have been executed after the cupola was complete and in or before 1444 when the building of the lantern was under way. The second support for this hypothesis is historical. As noted earlier, the King of Naples was represented at a peace conference summoned by the Pope in Siena in March 1444, and this was very possibly the occasion of the commissioning of the book. But the artistic interest of the Codex is greater still — it is an imaginative achievement of great complexity — and it may be wise at this point to turn its pages and read the illustrations.

* * *

31. Italian, mid-fourteenth-century: *Dante and Beatrice on the mount of Purgatory*, *Paradiso I* (Bibliothèque de l'Arsenal, Paris).

32. Venice, c. 1370: *Dante invoking Apollo*, *Paradiso I* (Biblioteca Marciana, Venice).

At the end of the *Purgatorio* Virgil, who had guided Dante through the first two Cantiche, vanishes, and is replaced by a new guide, Beatrice. The roles of Virgil and Beatrice are very different; Virgil is an expositor, whereas Beatrice is a superior intelligence. She is Dante's muse, an instructress who explains the mysteries of nature, the structure of the heavens, the phased ascent from earth to the celestial empyraean. Most early illustrators of the first Canto of the *Paradiso* represent Beatrice and Dante in conversation on the mount of Purgatory. But one late fourteenth century Venetian manuscript breaks free of this convention, and depicts, in a rudimentary fashion, the great invocation to Apollo with which the poem starts. Giovanni di Paolo does so too (f. 129r.). In an open meadow with a convex horizon are two mountain peaks. One of the Commentaries which the artist is likely to have known tells us

31

32

p.71

that Mount Parnassus 'avea due corni, cioè due colli,' and Dante indeed in the poem alludes to them metaphorically in speaking to Apollo:

Infino a qui l'un giogo di Parnaso
assai mi fu; ma or con amendue
m'e uopo intrar ne l'aringo rimaso.

In front is the tree into which Daphne was transformed, the laurel ('tuo diletto legno'), and beside it stands Apollo, with a raven under his feet, proffering to the kneeling poet two laurel wreaths. For the *Ottimo Commento* Apollo represented wisdom, radiating divine and human virtue, and this is intimated in the miniature by his crown of laurel and the gilding of his Roman armour. The poet begs Apollo to enter into his breast and breathe there as when he drew Marsyas from the sheath of his limbs. This is the subject of the right half of the miniature, where Marsyas is seen lying on the ground, his body scarred by the god's knife but not yet flayed. Further back is a belt of trees, in front of which a naked orange figure (sometimes interpreted as a second Marsyas and sometimes as Pan) is shown playing a flute. In the sky the nine Muses look down at the scene.

p.72 The two succeeding miniatures are less homogeneous and less poetical. In the first (f. 130r.) Beatrice (who here appears for the first time) leads Dante in what the poem describes as rapid flight ('ma folgore, fuggendo il proprio sito, non corse come tu ch'ad esso riedi') towards a winged boy, 'amor che'l ciel governi', standing in a planetary symbol of nine brightly lit concentric circles ('quei che puote/ avesse il ciel d'un altro sole addorno') casting its rays downwards on the sea of being beneath. Dante explains that in Beatrice's company he has suffered the same change of identity as Glaucus when after eating grass he became a sea god. On the left of the scene we see Glaucus, in course of metamorphosis, on a small island, fishing and, half-immersed in water, three sea gods, Proteus, Triton and Milcerta, who, according to the *Ottimo Commento*, welcomed him. Across the sea of being, from the centre to the right, are silhouettes of animals ('le creature che son fore/d'intelligenza') and two naked human figures lit by divine rays ('quelle c'hanno intelletto e amore'). In the sky on the left a smaller circular planetary symbol illustrates an earlier reference to the sun in Aries and to the four moral and three theological virtues.

p.74 Unexpectedly in the left half of the next scene (f. 131r.) Beatrice disappears and Dante, propelled by Minerva's golden breath, takes off into the air accompanied by Apollo, who points to an embossed star beside the Muses, the Great Bear. This is a literal rendering of the lines: 'Minerva spira, e conducemi Appollo, e nove Muse mi dimostran l'Orse'. Beneath Minerva is a boat rowing to the right, the little bark which is warned not to follow Dante's journey. Could it do so, Dante continues, its crew would be as astonished as were the Argonauts when they saw Jason in Colchis following a plough drawn by wild bulls.

Above: At the foot of the first page of the Yates-Thompson codex of the *Divine Comedy* are the arms of King Alfonso of Naples (Aragon quartering Hungary, Anjou and Jerusalem).

Overleaf: Page 38. The opening of Canto V, f. 136v (a left-hand page), showing one of the floriated initials with which each Canto begins.

Page 39. The opening of the last Canto, XXXIII, f. 189r (a right-hand page) which begins with St. Bernard's famous prayer to the Virgin and is therefore given a particularly elaborate initial. (See p. 186 for a facsimile reproduction of the miniature).

Page 40. The first page of the *Paradiso* (f. 129r), with the first of Giovanni di Paolo's illustrations at the foot (see p. 71). The historiated initial, showing Christ standing in benediction in a golden chariot drawn by an eagle, flanked by the symbols of the Evangelists and with Adam and Eve beneath him, is not by Giovanni di Paolo but by the illustrator of the *Inferno* and *Purgatorio*, Vecchietta.

o uo sauer se luom poso disfarmi
auoti manchi si conaltri biem
chala uostra stetera nõ sian parui

eatrice mi guardo cogliochi pieni
de sauille damor cosi diuini
che uinta mia uirtute diele reni

quasi mi pdei cogliochi chini
Capitolo. v. doue solue una quistione premessa nel prece
dente cap. et amaestra li xpiani circa luoti entra nel cie
lo di mercurio. e qui comincia la seconda
parte di questa cantica.

Io ti fiameggio nel caldo damore
oila dal modo chenterra si uede
si che deluiso tuo uincel ualore

onta mirauigliar che cio procede
da pfecto ueder che comapnde
cosi nel ben applõ mouel pede

o ueggio ben si come gia risplende
nellintellecto to leterna luce
che uista sola senpramor accende

saltra cosa uostra amor seduce
nõe se nõ diquella alchun uestigio
mal cognosciuto che qui triluce

u uuo sauer se con altro fuigio
pmanco uoto si puo render tanto
che lanima assiguri dalitigio

i comincio beatrice questo canto
et si comuom che suo parlar nõ speza
cõtinuo cosil processo santo

o magior duon che dio psua largeza
fesse creato et ala sua bontate
piu cõformato et quel che ei piu appreeza

u dela uolũta la libertate
di che le creature intellingenti
et tucte et sole et furo et son dotate

Vergine madre fillia del tuo fillio
humile et alta piu che creatura
termine fisso deterno consillo
Tu se colei che lumana natura
nobilitasti sichel tuo factore
no disdegno difarsi sua factura
Nel uentre tuo siraccese lamore
plo cui caldo neleterna pace
cosi e germinato questo fiore
Qui se anoi meridiana face
dicaritade et giuso intra mortali
se disperanza fontana uiuace
Donna se tanto grande et tanto uali
che qual uuol gra et adte no ricorre
sua disianza uuol uolar santali
La tua benignita no pur soccorre
achi dimanda ma molte fiate
liberamente aldimandar precorre
Inte misericordia inte pietate
inte magnificentia inte saduna
quantunque in creatura e dibontate
Orquesti che dalinfima alachuna
dellunuerso infinqui auedute
leuite spiritali aduna aduna
Supplica adte pergratia diuirtute
tanto che possa colliochi leuarsi
piu alto uerso lultima salute
Et io che mai pmio ueder nonarsi
piu chio fo plisuoi tucti miei peghi
tipriego et prego che no sieno scarsi
Perche tu ogni nube lidisleghi
disua mortalita coprieghi tuoi
sichel somo piacer lisidispieghi
Ancor tipriego regina che puoi
cio che tu uuoi cheli conserui sani
dopo tanto ueder laffecti suoi
Vinca tua gratia imouimeti humani
uedi beatrice conquati beati
pli miei peghi tichiudon lemani

ominicia la terza cantica dila
comedia di dante aldighieri
defirenze chiamata paradiso nella
quale tracta debeati e dilla celestiale
gloria e di meriti e premy di santi
e diuidise in noue parti sicome lo
inferno canto primo nello cui prin
cipio lautore prohemiza Alla seque
te cantica e sono nello alimento
dillo fuogo e beatrice solue allo au
tore una questione nello quale cato
lautore promecte di tractare le
cose diuine inuocando la scientia
poetica cioe apollo idio dilla sapia

La gloria de cholui che tucti moue
pluniuerso penietre risplende
in una pte piu et men altroue
Nel ciel che piu dela sua luce prnde
fuio et uiddi cose che redire
nesa nepo chi delassu descende
Per chappresando se alsuo desire
nostro intellecto si profunda tanto
che dietro lamimoria no puo ire
Veramte quato del regnio santo
nella mia mente puoti far tisoro
sira ora materia del mio canto
O buon apollo alultimo laboro
fame del tuo valor si facto uaso
come dimandi dar lamatalloro
In fino aqui lun gioco diparnaso
assai mi fu ma or con anbendui
me huopo intrar nellaringo rimaso
Intra nel pecto mio et spira tue
si come qn marsia trahesti
della uagina delle menbre sue
O diuina uirtu se mite presti
tanto che lonbra del beato regnio
segnata nel mio capo manifesti

This episode is shown in the lower left hand corner of the miniature. A diagonal line of cloud ('Parev a me che nube ne corpisse/lucida, spessa, solida e pulita') separates it from the inspired right side of the miniature, where Dante and Beatrice are shown flying across an Alpine landscape to the distant heaven of the moon. The crescent of the moon is lighted on the left – the *Ottimo Commento* compares its colour to 'latte candida' or unadulterated milk – and shaded on the right, to illustrate Dante's enquiry as to the 'segni bui' appearing on its surface.

In the latter part of the same Canto Beatrice explains the relation between the moon and sun and the principle of reflected light. For Giovanni di Paolo (f. 132r.), as for earlier illustrators, the account presented difficulties that were soluble only through juxtaposition of isolated passages. On the left Dante and Beatrice hover over two youths working at a forge. p.75 This reference is to a line in which Beatrice compares the Intelligence which controls the movement of the planets to a coppersmith whose hammering defines the form of the artefact on which he works. In the centre is a scene popular in earlier Dante manuscripts, in which a standing figure sees his own reflection in three mirrors set at different distances illuminated by a candle at his back. The candle – it is the size of a Paschal candle – is represented realistically with guttering wax. To the right a further scene illustrates the way in which under the warmth of the sun (once more depicted as it is shown on f. 130r.) the contents of a cloud descends as snow on to the ground beneath. In the centre above is a diagram – presumably drawn out by an astronomer – of the sun blocked by the dense surface of the moon in a solar eclipse.

With the first miniature of the third Canto (f. 133r.), one of the most magical in the p.76 whole book, we return from exposition to narrative. The scene is dominated by the crescent of the moon in which there float the figures of two nuns, Piccarda de' Donati and the Empress Costanza, with three of the naked souls or spirits to which Dante repeatedly refers. The foremost nun raises her hand in greeting to Dante and Beatrice, who is shown on this occasion not in full length but emerging from a cloud. Beneath, before a distant landscape, are small figures illustrating two of the similes in Dante's text. The first describes how the outlines of faces appear faint, like a pearl worn on the forehead, when seen through water or coloured glass. On the left is a youth holding a piece of coloured glass and on the right is Narcissus inspecting his own image in a well. The latter refers to the story of Narcissus 'a quel ch'accese amor tra l'omo e 'l fonte.' A sun heating the poet's breast with love shines on his chest. In the next miniature (f. 134r.) we descend from heaven to the earthly lives of p.77 Piccarda and Costanza and the circumstances that compelled them to break their vows. On the left is Piccarda 'giovinetta' in a white shift entering her convent, and in the centre she and Costanza are wrenched (one by her brother, the other by the Emperor's son Conrad) from their convent doors. The right half of the scene is extraneous to Dante's poem. It shows a crowned figure with the arms of Aragon at his feet, supervising the destruction of a city wall. Though no such incident is described in the *Paradiso*, a historical gloss is added in the *Ottimo Commento* which records that 'Federigo II fu il secondo genito della casa di Suave; Currado re, suo filgiuolo, nel 1251 prese la corona di Sicilia, e disfece le mura di Napoli.' This scene must have been included to give pleasure to the patron for whom the manuscript was destined.

p.79

The subject of Canto IV is not readily susceptible of illustration. The poem addresses two problems in Dante's mind that Beatrice resolves. How, he asks, can merit be diminished by acts done under compulsion? Reading bewilderment written on his face, Beatrice soothes him, as Daniel soothed Nebuchadnezzar, by explaining the nightmare by which he was haunted. The scene of Nebuchadnezzar's dream fills the left half of the miniature (f. 135r.). It shows the bedroom of the sleeping King with, above his bed, the mysterious vision by which he was pursued. In front stands Daniel interpreting the dream. Though it is no more than alluded to by Dante, the vision of a figure made of gold, silver, iron and clay, is described in some detail in the *Ottimo Commento*, and this is once more the source from which the scene derives. In the upper right hand corner is a radiant circle surrounded by cherubim, in which are seated Moses, Samuel and Saint John the Baptist. Just as they, Beatrice explains, are always shown with human features, which are apprehensible by sense perception, the archangels Michael, Gabriel and Raphael are likewise portrayed in human form. The three archangels, with heads turned back to Daniel, appear in the foreground on the right.

p.83

The second illustration to this Canto (f. 136r.) deals with strength of will, but does so through analogy. Plato, Dante reminds us, mistakenly claimed in the *Timaeus* that on death the soul returned to its own star. On the extreme left he is seen pointing with raised arm to a naked figure flying towards a star. There follow, here as in the poem, two depictions of the power of absolute will: St Lawrence on his grille and Mucius Scaevola burning his hand before Lars Porsena and lastly, as an example of misdirected will, Alcmaeon slaying his elderly mother in fulfilment of a vow to his father which he should never properly have made. The anecdotic treatment of these four incidents lends the miniature a sense of triviality, or would do so but for the continuous ascending landscape at the back.

p.85

The next scene (f. 137r.), the first of Canto V, is dominated by the Heaven of the Moon, with the standing figures of Dante silhouetted against its lighted surface and Beatrice silhouetted in reflected light against the darker surface opposite. The two figures are drawn with greater care than those in the preceding miniature, and hint for the first time at the intimate relationship between them that is implicit in Dante's text. 'I see well,' says Beatrice, 'how already shines in thy intellect the eternal light, which, when seen alone, ever kindles love.' The doctrine of free will is elaborated in four scenes below. One results from a misunderstanding of a line in the poem alluding to the sacrificial practice of the Hebrews; another shows St Peter holding two gold and silver keys with a naked child kneeling before him (a symbol of obedience to the church); in the third Jephtha, in fulfilment of an illicit vow, is seen stabbing his daughter; and in the fourth Agamemnon, in armour, sacrifices Iphigenia. Especially beautiful are the pallid mountains against which each group is set.

When, in the next illumination (f. 138r.), Dante and Beatrice, her coif billowing in the breeze, approach the Heaven of Mercury, the narrative becomes more lucid and direct. The planet is once more represented as a series of concentric circles, which, like the Moon in the preceding miniature, break the upper frame. Mercury, a naked youth surrounded by seven flying souls, is shown with arms extended greeting his two visitors. Beatrice, says Dante at this point, becomes so joyful that her radiance seems to illuminate the planet. Beneath are two independent scenes, the first of which follows immediately on the preceding reference to Iphigenia. Christians, exhorts Beatrice, unlike pagans, have the consistency of the New Testament and of the Pope to guide their conduct, and this should suffice for their salvation. In the centre at ground level is a Pope holding out two open books to a group of youths standing in front of him. The second occurs twenty lines later, when Dante compares the countless splendours attracted to Beatrice to fish in a pond rising to the surface in the hope of being fed. It is this simile that is illustrated. The passage is explained in the *Ottimo Commento* and in Giovanni di Paolo's miniature is represented by what must have been a common feature of life in the fifteenth century, a stew for storing fish. The artistic interest of the scene rests in its landscape which rises diagonally from the lower left corner to a median point on the right side. The expedient of imbalance is used, as in other scenes, to carry the eye forward to the following page.

p.87

When the page is turned (f. 139r.), the Heaven of Mercury is occupied by the Emperor Justinian standing on five volumes of the Pandects, in which, under divine inspiration, he purified the law, removing ordinances which were oppressive or irrelevant. At one time a monophysite, he was, he explains, convinced by Pope Agapetus of the dual nature of Christ. The Emperor is shown again on the extreme right kneeling before the Pope. In the centre the imperial standard, Dante's 'sacrosanto segno', is carried through two city gates. The first is that of Rome, identified by the pyramid of Cestius, and the second that of Byzantium. The bearers are Aeneas in Roman armour and the Emperor Constantine. The other historical allusions in the Canto are ignored. In the next scene the figure of Justinian is replaced by that of Romeo, whose 'noble work was ill rewarded', represented as a pilgrim in the constellation and as a beggar beneath. Instrumental in arranging the marriage of the daughters of Raymond Berengar of Provence to the Kings of France and England, the Earl of Cornwall and Charles of Anjou, Romeo was slandered by members of the Provençal court and disgraced on charges of dishonesty. The content of the bottom of the miniature is

p.88

p.91

historical. On the right is Romeo reduced to penury, and on a bench are seated the Count's four daughters with their husbands, on two of whose shields the correct arms are replaced by those of Aragon.

p.93   The illustrative level is raised in Canto VII (f. 141r.), where Justinian resumes his place, this time kneeling on the Pandects, as he describes the mystery of the Redemption. A craggy landscape beneath the feet of Dante and Beatrice gives way in the centre to the naked figures of Adam and Eve. What is represented in this scene is the Fall, not the Expulsion from Paradise. To the right is the first act of redemption, the Annunciation, with the Angel genuflecting to the kneeling Virgin in a simple tabernacle very different from the elaborate structure shown in Giovanni di Paolo's predella panel of the scene, and on the extreme right is its conclusion, Christ on the Cross with blood pouring from his hands and side. Set at an angle to the picture space, the Crucifixion confronts the figures in the Fall. All three were scenes the artist had painted many times, but here, treated as parts of a single programme, they register with great emotional force.

p.97   There is by exception no second illustration to Canto VII, presumably because the last hundred lines defied reduction to visual terms. With Canto VIII, however, the principle of dual illustration is reintroduced. On the right of the first miniature Beatrice places her hand on Dante's shoulder as she points to the Heaven of Venus, a radiant star in the upper corner of the scene. The sky, with its light horizontal clouds, and the calm sea beneath it are treated with enchanting delicacy. A little to the left of centre is an island on which four men kneel before a temple housing a naked Venus with two children. The Venus is the 'bella Ciprigna' of the poem and one of the children is Cupid ('ma Dïone onoravano e Cupido'). But there is no reference in the *Paradiso* to a second child. Its presence is, however, described in the *Ottimo Commento* which explains that Venus had 'suo singolare tempio' on the island of Cyprus, and that she bore two children, Amor and Cupid. 'Onde nota,' the passage reads, 'che li poeta secondo la credenza paganica attribuiscono a Venere due figliuoli, Amore e

p.98   Cupidine, per due suoi atti che di lussuria muovono.' The next scene is less poetical. The Heaven of Venus, which was first visible as a star, is now a concentric circle emitting golden rays, portrayed as though it were at some distance from the front plane of the scene. Its occupant is Charles Martel, Vicar of Naples and King of Hungary, who describes the territory over which he might have ruled. He had visited Florence a year before his death at the age of twenty-four and may have been familiar with Dante's early poems in the *De Convivio*. Below is an historical event referred to in the poem, the Sicilian Vespers (1282) when the French were evicted from Palermo by the forces of Peter III of Aragon. In this curious example of mini-history Palermo is defended by Aeneas and the invading forces are three men, two of whom carry the arms of Aragon. To the right is an empty boat, the 'barca carcata' referred to in the text, and in the distance is Mount Etna with its 'nascente solfo'.

In the first miniature of Canto IX (f. 144r.) the Heaven of Venus is occupied by the elegant figure of Cunizza da Romano, sister of the tyrant Ezzelino III da Romano, who in the early thirteenth century controlled much of north-east Italy. After a chequered career — she married four times and enjoyed a self-indulgent life — she resided in old age in Florence, whence in 1265 she granted freedom to her brother's and her father's slaves. Her presence in the Heaven of Venus, she explains to Dante, results from the influence which Venus exercised over her life. She makes no apology for her misdemeanours ('qui refulgo/perché mi vinse il lume d'esta stella;/ma lietamente a me medesma indulgo/la cagion di mia sorte, e non mi noia'). Below are the warring cities of Padua, Treviso, Feltre and Ferrara, backed by the sharp contours of a mountain range. The planet in this scene emits no rays, but in the following illustration (f. 145r.) it is once more represented as it was in the miniature of Charles Martel. Here the speaker is Folco the troubadour who, after his wife's death, became a Cistercian and Bishop of Toulouse. Cunizza is shown standing behind him. In this Canto there are a number of classical and other allusions which Giovanni di Paolo might have been expected to depict. Instead the subject is central to the Canto, Folco's great denunciation of the Florentines:

p.99
p.100

> La tua città, che di colui è pianta
> che pria volse le spalle al suo fattore
> e di cuí è la 'nvidia tanto pianta
> produce e spande il maladetto fiore
> c'ha disviate le pecore e li agni,
> però che fatto ha lupo del pastore.

To right of centre is a view of Florence, showing the Duomo without its lantern and the Campanile, the Palazzo della Signoria and a gateway, perhaps the Porta di Balla. Over the gate and on a wall to the right appears the lily of Florence. From a tower the devil, with his back to the Duomo, pours coins from a money bag into the hands of a Pope standing with his Cardinals on the extreme right. This scene is not illustrated in any other manuscript and manifests the anti-Florentine bias endemic in Siena.

With Canto X (f. 146r.) Dante and Beatrice approach the Heaven of the Sun. Once more a series of concentric circles, the Sun is of exceptional brilliance, throwing out thin golden rays into the sky above and pouring heavier rays on the serene landscape beneath. Those directed downwards are broken as they approach the earth. The scene illustrates the life-giving potency of sunlight:

p.103

> Lo ministro maggior del la natura,
> che del valor del ciel lo mondo imprenta
> e col suo lume il tempo ne misura.

p.104   The next miniature (f. 147r.) shows, in a flattened semi-circle, the interior of the sun, whose rays once more descend to a shallow strip of landscape at the base. In the upper half Dante and Beatrice encounter two Dominican theologians, Thomas Aquinas and Albertus Magnus. All four of the flying figures are set horizontally. Dante's hands are crossed, but Beatrice, with her right index finger, points down to ten seated figures, who include, on the extreme left, with a tonsure, the Venerable Bede, St Augustine and, presumably, Isidore of Seville and Dionysius the Areopagite. The crowned figure of Solomon appears to the right of the central group, and at his side are three laymen who likewise hold open books, Boethius, Gratian and Peter Lombard, with, on the extreme right, Richard of Saint Victor and Siger of Brabant. The heads are treated generically and are not differentiated.

p.105   In the next scene by contrast the radiant heaven fills the whole height of the miniature (f. 148r.). In it St Thomas Aquinas, depicted in flight, points down to the figures of Saints Dominic and Francis, both standing on winged seraphim. Across the sky run lines of cloud casting their shadow on the hills beneath. As in the two previous miniatures the responses of Beatrice are described with special care. The presence of seraphim beneath the feet of the two Saints is a literal illustration of Dante's lines:

L'un fu tutto serafico in ardore;
l'altro per sapienza in terra fue
di cherubica luce uno splendore.

p.106   In the centre of the next miniature to Canto XI (f. 149r.) the young St Francis, vowed to poverty, kneels naked before the Bishop of Assisi. The setting is a reconstruction of Dante's description of the Umbrian countryside. To the left on its hill is the convent of San Francesco at Assisi with Santa Maria degli Angeli in the valley beneath. Across the middle runs the river Tupino, and on the right is the 'colle eletto dal beato Ubaldo', Gubbio. With

p.109   the first scene of Canto XII (f. 150r.) the size of the Heaven of the Sun is once more reduced, and St Thomas Aquinas gives way to St Bonaventure, who describes the apostolate of St Dominic in Spain. The town of Calaroga 'non molto lungi al percuoter de l'onde,' here shown beside a sea that fills the lower left corner of the scene. The Saint, writes Dante, 'ne li sterpi eretici percosse/ l'impeto suo, più vivamente quivi/ dove le resistenze eran più grosse,' and in the miniature he is shown on the right adjuring a group of bearded heretics whose types recall the Jews in Giovanni di Paolo's predella panels of the Crucifixion. A page later

p.111   (f. 151r.) we return to the interior of the Heaven, again represented as a radiant semi-circle with a shallow strip of landscape beneath. This time the presiding figure is St Bonaventure. Beneath are shown St Francis and eleven companions, who include two early Franciscans, Illuminato and Agostino, Gioacchino da Fiore, and Saints John Chrysostom, Anselm and Augustine.

From this apotheosis of the mendicant order we descend abruptly to mythology (f. 152r.). 'Imagini,' writes Dante in the fourth and fifth tercets of Canto XIII,

la bocca di quel corno
che si comincia in punta de lo stelo
a cui la prima rota va dintorno,
aver fatto di sè due segni in cielo,
qual fece la figliuola di Minoi
allora che sentì di morte il gelo.

Modern Dante commentators explain these lines as describing twenty-four stars disposed as a double Ariadne's Crown, but for Giovanni di Paolo they contained no astrological allusion, and his scene shows two islands in a tranquil sea, on one of which Theseus in gold p.113
armour is represented slaying the Minotaur, while on the other, Naxos, the deserted Ariadne is awakened from the sleep of death by love. A similar winged figure of Amor occurs again some pages later in the context of the story of Hippolytus. There is no reference to the Minotaur, here represented as a centaur, in Dante's text. It has been suggested that 'for both scenes the artist probably used a pictorial source available to him', but they have the arbitrary character of free invention and no such source is known. The pale green sea, the yellow horizon and the distant mountains are treated with enchanting freshness. The second miniature in this Canto (f. 153r.), from which Dante and Beatrice are also absent since they p.114
are not participants, is once more dominated by the Heaven of the Sun, breaking the upper frame and pouring its rays down not on a landscape but on horizontal lines of cloud. Seated on cloud are three figures mentioned in close conjunction in the text, Christ, Adam and Solomon.

This chain of ideas extends to Canto XIV, where Beatrice, on Dante's behalf, asks Solomon whether at the resurrection of the dead the light of risen bodies will not be so intense as to hurt the eyes. The relevant illumination (f. 154r.) shows the resurrected bodies bathed p.115
in light genuflecting as they rise through the cloud-covered sky. The illumination seems to be based on knowledge, perhaps at second hand, of Fra Angelico's well-known panel of the Last Judgment, then at Santa Maria degli Angeli in Florence, where the graves from which the dead emerge are represented perspectivally as dark rectangles in a marble pavement. Giovanni di Paolo's miniature depicts two sarcophagi and six rectangular graves distributed without regard to any unitary perspective scheme. There is no second illustration to this Canto.

By this time the Heaven of the Sun has given way to that of Mars, the base of which is visible at the top. When the whole Heaven appears in the fifteenth Canto (f. 155r.), it does so p.117
over a hilly landscape and is occupied by Dante's great-great-grandfather Cacciaguida. The

narrative starts in the lower left corner with an unintelligible image of two recumbent naked figures, perhaps Dante's earliest ancestors, one, a man, sleeping on the ground, and the other, a woman, seated, as though awakened by the heavenly rays. Before Cacciaguida identifies himself, Dante inserts a reference to Virgil's magnificent account of the greeting offered in the Elysian fields by the shade of Anchises to his son Aeneas. This scene is illustrated in the lower right hand corner of the miniature. The analogy between the two encounters is reflected in the pose of Cacciaguida, who is shown with head turned back to Dante but with his right hand pointing to the scene below. The tree-filled Tuscan landscape is repeated in

p.119 the next miniature (f. 156r.), where Cacciaguida, now facing Dante, explains their relationship. Ignoring the passage in which Cacciaguida contrasts the Florence of the past with the Florence of Dante's day, the miniature instead moves to the extreme end of the Canto, where Cacciaguida describes how the Emperor Conrad girded him as a knight (this scene takes place on the left in the courtyard of a castle which cannot be identified), how he joined the Second Crusade, and how he was slain by the Mohammedans. The last event is represented by two vigorous figures at the right.

Dante's dialogue with Cacciaguida continues in the single miniature devoted to the
p.120 sixteenth Canto (f. 157r.), which deplores the growth of Florence through its incorporation of neighbouring towns and villages and of the castles which were once associated with the Florentine nobility. Six of these are portrayed at the base of the miniature, one, possibly Florence itself, larger than the rest and two on a much smaller scale. All six conform to a simple structural scheme in which the forward faces are the point of juncture of two walls. Cacciaguida's prophecy of Dante's future exile is the subject of the two following
p.121 miniatures. In the first (f. 158r.), one of the most vivid narratives in the whole book, Cacciaguida, in the Heaven of Mars, stands in the upper right corner with one hand on his chest. 'As Hippolytus left Athens, by reason of his pitiless and perfidious stepmother,' he warns Dante, 'so from Florence must you depart.' In the left we see the grief stricken figure of Hippolytus with one hand to his face leaving the gate of Athens. Inside the city sits his step-mother Phaedra seduced by a flying figure of Amor. To the right Hippolytus appears once more, dying beneath the wheels of his chariot at Troezen. The conduct of Phaedra is censured by Dante in the line: 'per la spietata e perfida noverca,' but the rare scene of the death of Hippolytus is due not to Dante but to the *Ottimo Commento*, which repeats Ovid's account of Hippolytus driving his chariot along the sea shore and of the vision which caused his horses to take fright. In the miniature the chariot is depicted as a rustic waggon. The gate
p.125 of Florence to the left of the next scene (f. 159r.) is somewhat larger than that of Athens but recedes at the same angle into the picture space. Its identity is established by the customary lily and by a view of the Duomo which is closely similar to that used on f. 145r. Dante is portrayed in profile as the counterpart of Hippolytus, but to establish that his departure from

Florence was involuntary a citizen is shown thrusting him through the gate. The right half of the scene is set in Verona, where Dante, now a guest of Can Grande della Scala, sits in a loggia looking over the river Adige, with one hand pressed sorrowfully to his face. From a narrative standpoint these are two of the finest and most sensitive of the illuminations.

The next five miniatures, devoted to the Heaven of Jupiter, have no narrative character. Dante's concern in Cantos XVIII, XIX and XX is with concepts, and in illumination these could be clarified only through pattern. A moral breakdown of their structure provided by the *Ottimo Commento* was evidently fundamental for the illustrations. The Heaven of Jupiter, explains the commentary, is filled with 'anime che furono disposte a giustizia,' and the colour of the heaven is 'chiaro a resplendente, onde è argento, ed a similitudine di latte candida.' For St Augustine, the commentary reminds us, justice had two aspects, to reject evil and to do good. Justice, 'secondo che dice Tullio nel primo libro della Rettorica, è abito d'animo,' while for Macrobius, 'Giustizia è osservare a ciascuno suo diritto.' The first scene in Canto XVIII shows the Heaven of Jupiter, with the armed figure of Jupiter standing inside it. Projecting from the sphere is the head of Cacciaguida. This is the subject of a note in the *Ottimo Commento* that reads: 'Qui rientrò il detto messer Cacciaguida nel proprio luogo, nel quale mostrò in che grado elle era tra costoro: ma l'Autore non lo scrive, ma lascialo allo intelletto del lettore.' Cacciaguida describes a tree or cross composed of spirits who on earth had earned great renown. To the right this is represented by a radiant cross with eight armed warriors headed by Joshua and including Judas Maccabaeus and Charlemagne. The cross is represented somewhat in the fashion of a number of fourteenth century illuminated Dante manuscripts, but the figures who compose it are here treated with greater freedom and the diagonal gold rays invest them with a truly visionary quality. The next scene is more ambiguous. The heaven is filled by a naked female figure that is sometimes explained as the love that Dante sees sparkling 'in quella giovial facella' Beatrice, but is more probably the muse Euterpe, the 'diva Pegasëa' whom Dante invokes in the poem as his aid in describing the visions he experiences. On the right is the Eagle of Justice with head turned in profile, protecting with his wings ten naked spirits with linked hands ranged in two lines beneath. This part of the miniature evidently illustrates the opening of the nineteenth Canto:

p.127

p.130

Parea dinanzi a me con l'ali aperte
la bella image che nel dolce frui
lieti facevan l'anime conserte.

A similar group of souls dancing joyfully in concentric circles appears in a late fourteenth century *Paradiso* in the Morgan Library.

The Eagle of Justice, with wings and body constructed of just souls, is commonly represented as Dante describes it in Canto XIX, but never with such authority as in the p.131   present book (f. 162r.). The eagle fills the whole height of the field. Its body is set frontally, and its legs are shown apart forming a pyramid that is repeated in its open wings. The width of the miniature is reduced to emphasise the eagle's size. There follow, seated in a semi‑circle (f. 163r.) the Unjust Rulers. 'What will the Persians (heathens),' Dante asks, 'say to your king when they shall see that volume opened in which are written all the dispraises of them?' In the centre is the Book of Judgment. All the Unjust Rulers save one are crowned with an imperial not a royal crown, and though we know from Dante's text the names of a number of them – they include the Emperor Albert of Austria, Philip IV of France who debased the French currency, and Charles II of Naples – there are several who cannot be identified. The heads of a number of the rulers are turned apprehensively towards the book.

     At the beginning of the twentieth Canto Dante once more describes the eagle, which produces sounds that at first are like the murmurings of a river but progressively become louder like a wind traversing a hollow pipe, and then issue through its beak as an intelligible

p.135   voice. In the resulting miniature it is no longer represented frontally, but is set diagonally across the field, with wings touching the margin at either side. On it there stand the diminutive figures of the five just rulers, David in the centre and with him Trajan, Hezekiah, the Emperor Constantine, and William the Good of Sicily. A sixth figure, that of the Trojan Ripheus, praised by Virgil as 'justissimus unus/ Qui fuit in Teucris, et servantissimus aequi', is omitted, seemingly because the reference in Dante was misread in the *Ottimo Commento*.

p.137   With the next illumination (f. 165r.) we move to Canto XXI and to the Heaven of Saturn. The Heaven, an opaque, blue grey sphere, supported by angels whose long wings stretch out round its circumference, is set in the upper right corner. In it stands Saturn, an austere bearded figure holding a scythe. In the fifth and sixth lines of the Canto Beatrice tells Dante that if she smiled on him he would be consumed by fire as was Semele by the majesty of Jupiter:

> 'Si io ridessi,'
> mi comminciò, 'tu ti faresti quale
> fu Semele, quando di cener fessi.'

This passage is the source of what is perhaps the most striking image in the whole volume, of Semele reduced to ashes, her yellow hair and pink dress concealed by pale green smoke and golden flames which rise like peacock's plumage from her side. The death of Semele is treated in the *Ottimo Commento* with the same emphasis accorded to it in the miniature, with a gloss taken from Ovid: 'Non vuole dire altro, se non la tua potenza, insufficiente a tanta luce, vorrebbe tutta meno, si come Semele, percussa dalla folgore di Giove, arse, e cenere divenne.' On the opposite side a ladder is held in place by angels. This is the 'scaleo eretto in suso' of Dante's vision, and the angels are the splendours or lights climbing up it:

Vidi anche per li gradi scender giuso
tanti splendor, ch'io pensai ch'ogne lume
che par nel ciel, quindi fosse diffuso.

In the Codex the following scenes conform to the sequence of the poem with the exception of the first scene of Canto XXI (f. 166r.) which depends from the *Ottimo Commento*, not from the *Paradiso*. The setting is Sicily; at the back is a mountain that may be intended as Vesuvius, and on the right is Etna in eruption. At the front, on yellow stools, are seated four Kings of Sicily, two of them inevitably with the arms of Aragon. An ideogram representing a town is repeated in the middle distance and at the front.

p.140

The next scene (f. 167r.) reverts to Dante's text, and is devoted to his encounter with St Peter Damian, who stands a little to the left of centre in the Heaven of Saturn. The passage opens with an account of the Appenines rising between the shores of Italy, which 'fanno un gibbo che si chiama Catria.' On the right of the miniature are the precipitous crags 'so high that the thunders sound far below' described by Dante. St Peter tells how his contemplative life was interrupted by promotion to the rank of Cardinal, and inveighs against the corruption of the church. Below are three separate episodes. In the first St Peter, accompanied by a tonsured novice, approaches a small convent building in the middle ground; in the second he is seated at the entrance to a cave with a cardinal's hat at his feet; and in the third he sits outside another conventual building. On the last occasion he is shown without a halo. It is not clear (and cannot indeed have been clear to Giovanni di Paolo) whether Dante's allusion to 'Peter the Sinner in the house of our Lady on the Adriatic shore' relates to the Saint himself or to a Bishop, Petrus Peccator, who founded the monastery of Santa Maria di Porto Fuori at Ravenna. The scene on the right may show St Peter himself before he became Cardinal and the scene in the centre the sanctity that he achieved when he returned to his pristine contemplative life.

p.141

The subject of the next miniature (f. 168r.) is the complementary career of St Benedict, who is seen, in three-quarter face, vested as an Abbot addressing Dante and Beatrice. His story, like that of St Peter Damian, is reduced to three scenes. In the first the Saint walks alone along a stony path; in the second he attacks a pagan temple; and in the third, with a novice as his companion, he sits outside the monastery of Monte Cassino. In the poem St Benedict describes how he 'withdrew the villages round about from the impious worship that seduced the world.' The *Ottimo Commento* elaborates these words with the gloss: 'cacciò la cultura degli idoli di quella montagna in sulla quale era il tempio d'Apollo,' and it is indeed a temple of Apollo that St Benedict is shown attacking in the illumination.

p.142

At the end of Canto XXII, in an inspired passage, Beatrice instructs Dante to look at the whole heavenly world that has been revealed to him. Gazing at the seven spheres he sees the earth ('questo globo/tal ch'io sorrisi del suo vil sembiante') and then the Planets, 'la figlia di Latona', that is the Moon; the child of Hyperion, that is the Sun; 'Maia e Dione', the mothers of Mercury and Venus; Jupiter between Mars and Saturn, as he 'circles with the eternal Twins'. For Giovanni di Paolo (f. 169r.) the problem was solved with a planetary symbol filling the whole height of the miniature containing Leda and the Gemini, in seven circles identified by colour as the planets. Beneath is a line of planetary deities, represented by the figures shown in the previous illuminations in the order not of Dante's poem but of the days of the week. On the left beneath the flying figures of Dante and Beatrice is the Sun, and to the right there stand in sequence the Moon, Mars, Mercury, Jupiter, Venus and Saturn.

p.145

Canto XXIII brings us to the Heaven of the Fixed Stars. In the first of a series of consecutive scenes (f. 170r.) Dante and Beatrice appear on the left, as spectators not participants, while to the right is a radiant circle edged with stars. In it a foreshortened Christ looks down on a band of kneeling naked figures, whose heads are raised to the light pouring down on them. The scene has as its source the lines in which Dante describes the light of the sun (that is, of Christ) kindling souls as the real sun kindles the natural world. A page later we reach a related but more complex scene (f. 171r.) in which the circle is enlarged and the Fixed Stars are replaced by ten angels standing on wisps of cloud. Within the circle is Christ holding the Old and New Testaments, and beneath him are the Virgin (posed frontally as though in an Assumption) and St Peter holding his gold and silver keys. This scene relates to the last lines of the Canto:

p.147
p.150

> Quivi triunfa, sotto l'alto Figlio
> di Dio e di Maria, di sua vittoria,
> e con l'antico e col novo concilio
> colui che tien le chiavi di tal gloria.

The two miniatures in Canto XXIV describe Dante's encounter with St Peter. The circle of Fixed Stars resumes its place, and in it (f. 172r.) is the Saint turned three-quarters to the left. In the first Dante is represented at an angle to the picture plane with his robe blown in folds across his hips, and the figure of Beatrice likewise takes on a new urgency. When Dante's interrogation is at an end, he makes his profession of faith (f. 173r.), and St Peter coming forward encircles him with a white cord in the presence of eight naked souls. On the right is a symbolic figure of Faith holding the cross. With Canto XXV (f. 174r.) Faith is succeeded by Hope and Charity in the form of winged angels in flight at either side. At the top of the circle on a single bench sit the Triumphant and the Suffering Christ. Beneath are two dancing figures ('vid'io lo schiarato splendore/ venire ai due, che si volgieno a nota') and the figures of Saints James and the young John the Evangelist. The head of St James appears

p.152
p.153
p.157

once more on the left, protruding from the Heaven addressing the virtue of Hope. At the bottom, outside the starry circle, the figure of Dante, turned inwards, kneels before each of the two apostles. Turning towards Beatrice, Dante is disturbed that he cannot see her, and in the miniature she is omitted from the scene. She reappears, however, in the next miniature (f. 175r.), where Dante encounters St John the Evangelist, now represented in old age not in p.158 youth. The moment of depiction may well be that at which St John, with the words 'My body is earth', denies the legend of his Assumption. Canto XXVI contains as its climatic point the vision of 'l'anima prima/ che la prima virtù creasse mai', Adam. Though Dante addresses Adam as 'padre antico' and though he is shown in other manuscripts as a venerable bearded figure, he is represented here (f. 176r.) as the heroic youth of the Expulsion p.159 from Paradise, not inappropriately since the poem deals with the nature of his sin and with the Fall. The eagerness with which Adam accosts Dante in the poem is faithfully reflected in the miniature. Adam is accompanied by five youths or members of his family. In the bottom left hand corner is the tree-crowned mount of Paradise with the customary four rivers emerging from it.

In the last illustration of the Heaven of the Fixed Stars (f. 177r.) St Peter reappears, p.161 pointing indignantly to the lower right corner of the scene, where a seated Pope hands a banner marked with the 'signaculo' of the papal keys to two soldiers 'che contra battezzati combattesse'. Behind them, in reference to Dante's 'lupi rapaci', crouches a wolf. A casque and papal bull illustrate the words 'privilegi venduti e mendaci'. Above is the Trinity, invoked in the first line of the Canto, depicted not in natural light but in red and gold. This depends from Dante's description:

> *Di quel color che per lo sole avverso*
> *nube dipigne da sera e da mane,*
> *vid'io allora tutto 'l ciel cosperso.*

The *Ottimo Commento* points out (as later commentators have also done) that St Peter's indignation is expressed in the poem by the literary device of repetition:

> *Quelli ch' usurpa in terra il luogo mio,*
> *il luogo mio, il luogo mio che vaca*
> *ne la presenza del Figliuol di Dio.*

In the miniature the open gesture of the Saint's left arm achieves the same effect. The three kneeling figures, seemingly children, illustrate the words, 'Fede e innocenza sono reperte/ solo ne' parvoletti'.

In Canto XXVIII Dante reaches the Primum Mobile. 'The nature of the universe, which holds the centre quiet and moves all the rest around it,' Beatrice explains, 'begins here p.162 as from its starting point.' In a green and gold circle edged with golden cherubim is a mappamondo of the earth (f. 178r.). Around it in the inner circle is the sea, depicted with a pattern of curved linear brushstrokes as though in rapid clockwise revolution. The image and the sense of movement it generates is a close approximation to the description at the beginning of the Canto, but has been mistakenly referred to a passage at the close of the Canto XXVII. In front of it is Christ the Redeemer, with feet superimposed on one of the supporting cherubim. His right arm is raised and his left hand extended, and his blue and yellow cloak is blown out at each side by the movement of the sphere. To us this image reads as one of startling originality, but in Siena its iconography would have been familiar since it occurs in an intarsia panel by Domenico di Niccolò dei Cori in a cycle of the Articles of the Creed in the chapel of the Palazzo Pubblico, where the central figure is God the Father and which carries the inscription 'Factorem celi et terre visibilium omnium et invisibilium.' It appears again in a miniature by Pellegrino di Mariano as the initial letter of 'In principio fecit Deus celum et terram,' where God the Father not the Redeemer is shown. Giovanni di Paolo's illumination is, from a creative standpoint, vastly superior to other representations of p.165 the kind. No less vivid is the following miniature (f. 179r.), where Dante and Beatrice are seen before a sphere composed of pale yellow and ochre rings in whose centre is a head emitting golden rays. The head is that of the wind god Boreas, and the scene illustrates two specific lines of Dante's poem:

Come rimane splendido e sereno
l'emisperio de l'aere, quando soffia
Borea da quella guancia ond'è più leno.

The third illustration to Canto XXVIII and the first to XXIX are dominated once more by the Trinity, in a variant of the cartoon employed in the scene of St Peter's denunciation of the papacy. In them the persons of the Trinity are differentiated by their haloes, circular in the case of God the Father, and rectangular with Christ and the Holy Ghost. In both Dante and Beatrice appear in their customary position on the left, but with the difference that in the second Beatrice is shown in horizontal not diagonal flight. In the bottom right corner of the p.166 first scene (f. 180r.) sits St Dionysius holding a book, 'lo libro de Angelica Jerarcia.' The passage illustrated is Beatrice's explanation of the angelic hierarchy. The long multi-coloured wings of the seraphim extend upwards on either side of the Trinity. In the foreground are three groups of three angels, differentiated by colour; they form half of a circle p.167 of lighter angels, of nine of which only the haloes are visible. The second scene (f. 181r.) illustrates the defeat, by Michael and Raphael, of the rebel angels who are thrust down to hell. This rare scene recurs on a panel in the Louvre by a follower of Simone Martini, in which the animated silhouettes of the falling angels foreshadow those in the illumination.

After these elevated and uncompromising miniatures, it is a welcome surprise to come on the following page (f. 182r.) to one of the allegorical digressions that had attracted Giovanni di Paolo in the earlier cantos of the poem. 'Ora si va,' writes Dante in condemnation of the preachers of his day:

> con motti e con iscede
> a predicare, e pur che ben si rida
> gonfia il cappuccio e più non si richiede.
> Ma tale uccel nel becchetto s'annida,
> che se 'l vulgo il vedesse, vederebbe
> la perdonanza di ch'el si confida:
> per cui tanta stoltezza in terra crebbe,
> che, sanza prova d'alcun testimonio,
> ad ogne promession si correrebbe.
> Di questo ingrassa il porco sant'Antonio
> e altri assai che sono ancor più porci,
> pagando di moneta sanza conio.

This passage is directed against preachers who fail to provide their congregations with a foundation of true doctrine, and instead 'go with jest and railleries to preach, and so long as there is a good laugh, the cowl puffs out, and no more is asked.' The scene is set in the open air against a low pink wall. An audience of three men and three women listen to the preaching of a friar, the three women with credulous attention while two of the men laugh at a joke made by the preacher. Clinging to the friar's back is a devil like those expelled from paradise. On the extreme right stands a swineherd with the symbol of greed, the 'porco di Sant'Antonio.' This is the only example in the entire series of illuminations of the talent Giovanni di Paolo manifests in his predella panels for recording scenes from daily life. p.171

One of the sublime passages of the *Paradiso* is Dante's description in Canto XXX of the river of light, its two banks painted with spring flowers. 'Faville vive' rise from the water and settle on the flowers like rubies mounted in gold, and then, as though drunk with the scent, plunge back into the stream. In the illumination (f. 183r.) beneath yet another representation of the Trinity, the child-like figures dive into the water and bathe there amid a profusion of lilies and wild flowers. Beatrice tells Dante to bend down and bathe his eyes in the water, and in at least one mid-fourteenth century manuscript he is shown doing this, but Giovanni di Paolo omits this scene, and instead Dante kneels in prayer on the river bank. In the following miniature (f. 184r.), also from Canto XXX, Dante and Beatrice are again in flight, as Beatrice displays the celestial city, a walled fortress with towers and crenellated walls, in appearance not unlike Monteriggioni near Siena. Inside it are two rows of tiered benches· p.172 p.173

33. Padua, early fifteenth-century: *Dante and Beatrice and the imperial throne, Paradiso XXX* (Seminario, Padua).

occupied by naked figures waiting for the Emperor's soul to take its place on a throne in the centre marked with the imperial eagle. The norm in fourteenth century illuminations of this

33 Canto was to omit the city and show the vacant throne alone.

In the Empyrean of the next to penultimate Canto of the *Paradiso* (XXXI), Beatrice relinquishes her role as Dante's mentor and returns to her place among the blessed. In the present volume, however, she reappears in three of the last four illuminations. In the first of them she reveals the mystic rose and explains the figures enclosed in it. The concept of a rose filled with human figures offered a descriptive challenge that earlier Dante illustrators tended

36 to evade. A mid-fourteenth century Emilian manuscript in the British Library shows the rose against the sky, with the heads of the figures named in the poem projecting from cliffs at

35 either side. In another miniature of the same date in the Bibliothèque de l'Arsenal the rose is represented geometrically with a large circle in the centre, and petals in the form of circles

34 round it. A Venetian manuscript in the Biblioteca Marciana reduces it to a central circle with sixteen schematic petals round it, on which small figures are superimposed. Giovanni

p.177 di Paolo treats it very differently (f. 185r.), since one of his interests was botany.

34, 35, 36. Three fourteenth-century illuminations of *The Celestial Rose*, *Paradiso XXXI*. Above left: Venice, late fourteenth-century (Biblioteca Marciana, Venice). Above right: Italian, mid-fourteenth-century (Bibliothèque de l'Arsenal, Paris). Below: Emilian or Paduan, mid-fourteenth-century (British Library, London).

In the early fifteenth century prolific artists often worked from model books. Giovanni di Paolo may have done so too, but the flowers in his panel paintings have a freshness and validity that can only have resulted from first hand study of plant forms over many years. Nature study was not limited to his early altarpieces. It continued throughout his life. A small *Madonna* in the Lindenau Museum at Altenburg has a painted frame filled with four long-stemmed pinks, each of which differs from the other three. In the 1450s a predella with scenes from the life of the Baptist, in London, has interstices filled with cut roses depicted in the same way. This practice recurs in a very late predella in the Siena gallery, and in two Madonnas of the same time, where the Virgin is seen in front of a rose hedge. When, therefore, he was confronted with the closing pages of the *Divine Comedy* what he envisioned was a real rose to which the figures were subordinate.

The scale of the rose described by Dante is very great. The 'milizia santa' feeding upon it, the angels descending like a swarm of bees to bring it nectar, form a cosmic vision which could be represented only if it were reduced to finite terms. Giovanni di Paolo's rose is relatively small, and recedes at an angle from the picture plane. At its centre is the Trinity (inspired no doubt by Dante's 'Oh trina luce che 'n unica stella/ scintillando a lor vista, sì li appaga') and nestling in its petals are nine angels. At the bottom are two sprigs of foliage. There follows (f. 186r.) a scene which, in the *Paradiso*, is explained by St Bernard:

vola con li occhi per questo giardino;
ché veder lui t'acconcerà lo sguardo
più al montar per lo raggio divino.
E la regina del cielo, ond'io ardo
tutto d'amor, ne farà ogne grazia,
però ch'i' sono il suo fedel Bernardo.

p.181   The miniature shows a flower-filled garden backed by a curved wood fence. In the centre, on the ground, the Virgin sits in profile, as in a Burgundian miniature, holding the Child and attended by five angels. On the right inside the paling of the garden kneels St Bernard in his Cistercian habit gazing intently at Dante opposite.

p.182   In the first miniature to Canto XXXII (f. 187r.) the rose reappears. The flower in this illumination is on a rather smaller scale, as though seen from a greater distance, and more foliage is shown. In the centre in place of the Trinity is the Virgin of Humility with Eve prostrate beneath her feet. The occupants of its petals are listed by Dante as a number of Old Testament figures (not depicted here) and Saints John the Baptist, Francis, Benedict and Augustine, with the representatives of the Old and New Law separated. In the miniature Dante's distinction between the categories of figures is ignored, and the identity of a number of them is changed. There are three female figures, St Anne below Eve and two unidentified figures aligned with her, and the male figures include, on either side of the Virgin, St Peter and the Baptist.

With the next miniature (f. 188r.) the vision of the rose undergoes a change; it is p.183 represented with fewer petals and on a larger scale, a close up view in which the lower petals are severed by the frame. The figures are larger than those in the earlier scene, and fill the petals in a more natural way. The stamen is occupied, not by the Virgin and Child, but by the scene of the Annunciation. Two of the three other figures are Moses and St Anne, and the third is St Bernard, Dante's guide in the closing Canto of the *Paradiso*. Under the guidance of Beatrice, Dante plucks at St Bernard's sleeve, asking the question:

> qual è quell' angel che con tanto gioeo
> guarda ne li occhi la nostra regina,
> innamorato sì che par di foco?

and the Saint's replies:

> perch' elli è quelli che portò la palma
> giuso a Maria, quando 'l Figliuol di Dio
> carcar si volse de la nostra salma.

This scene is less wide than the preceding miniature, and in the penultimate illumination (f. 189r.) the width is still further reduced. The subject is St Bernard's prayer at the opening of Canto XXXIII:

> Vergine Madre, figlia del tuo figlio,
> umile ed alta più che 'e creatura,
> termine fisso d'etterno consiglio,
> tu se' colei che l'umana natura
> nobilitasti sì, che 'l suo fattore
> non disdegnò di farsi sua fattura.

The Virgin sits on a marble bench which in turn rests on an inlaid marble platform. The p.186 angle of her head, and the cloak drawn over her shoulder, and the gesture of the Child repeat those of the Virgin in f. 187r. The right corner of the platform is masked by the standing figure of St Bernard who points with his right hand to the Virgin. His left hand rests on the head of Dante who is depicted as a timid supplicant before the Virgin's throne. The scene conveys a sense of emotional saturation that is carried through into the last illumination (f. 190r.). On the left is Dante with hands clasped in prayer, as Beatrice, once more in flight, p.189 places one hand on his head and with the other points to a vision of the Assumption of the Virgin surrounded by a mandorla of golden rays. The concluding verse of the *Paradiso* is an apostrophe of the Virgin, and it is appropriate that this last scene of the Codex should be represented by an image so central to the devotional life of the city in which the volume was produced. There is, however, on the right side of the same miniature a further scene. It illustrates the last of the great similes that punctuate the *Paradiso*:

> *Un punto solo m'è maggior letargo*
> *che venticinque secoli a la 'mpresa*
> *che fé Nettuno ammirar l'ombra d'Argo.*
> *Così la mente mia, tutta sospesa,*
> *mirava fissa, immobile e attenta,*
> *e sempre di mirar faceasi accesa.*

Neptune, rising from the water, raises his hand in wonder as Jason's boat, the Argo, lit by the radiance of the mandorla, casts its shadow forwards across the pale green sea.

*   *   *

The miniatures throughout this Codex mark a revolution in Dante illustration. They were planned as a visual interpretation of Dante's text in terms that readers of the *Paradiso* in the middle of the fifteenth century would understand. Giovanni di Paolo was a devout as well as a devotional artist. The only other substantial group of book illuminations by him that we know occurs in an Antiphonary commissioned for the Augustinian hermitage of Lecceto now in the Biblioteca Communale at Siena. The painted field in them is larger; the principal initial letters are four times as high as the Dante miniatures, and the splendid miniature of *Death on Horseback* is double the width and height of the *Paradiso* scenes. On this large scale the emotions of *Christ feeding the Sheep with Wheat* and *Christ drying the Eyes of the Apostles* could be defined more clearly than those of figures in the *Paradiso* illuminations. But what the *Paradiso* miniatures lack in definition is made up in movement and continuity. In any illustrated book the scenes must respond to the nature of the text, and from the very start the artist leaves us in no doubt that his illuminations are the record of a journey through space and time and an account of the spiritual growth of his protagonist.

There are three constants in the illuminations. The first is the structure of the universe represented by the spheres and sky. In a very literal sense the spheres dominate these illuminations. They could be looked at in the fifteenth century as we look at them to-day, as pattern or geometry. Part of their appeal rests on the relationship between the circles of the heavens and the rectangles of the fictive frames. The frames were solid and immutable, but the diameter of the spheres could be increased or reduced with a view not only to changing their effect as pattern but to indicating the notional space within the scene.

37
38

60

37, 38. Giovanni di Paolo: two
miniatures from an Antiphonary,
Death on Horseback and *Christ drying the
Eyes of the Apostles* (Biblioteca
Communale, Siena).

39. Giovanni di Paolo: *Last Judgment* (Pinacoteca Nazionale, Siena).

Nowadays the sky is the domain of weather-forecasters and meteorologists. But at the time this manuscript was illustrated it had a deeper significance. It was a zone of mystery, from which saints descended and to which human souls returned. The consistent portrayal of the sky throughout the miniatures is central to the narrative unity of the whole book. It is the carefully handled horizontal clouds that persuade us to accept the presence in one field of two discordant images (as with the conjunction of the Temple of Venus and Dante and Beatrice flying toward the moon) or some scene against which reason may rebel (like the Saved floating jubilantly above their graves). There are no clouds in the higher heavens save those serving as a faldstool for Dante, the only weighty human figure seen in them.

A second unifying factor is landscape. The most elaborate of the landscapes is the first, with its view of the twin peaks of Parnassus and the curved horizon that, in the artist's panel paintings, is used to indicate that the area shown is not a specific place but a segment of the world. Elsewhere the height and angle of the landscapes change constantly. In the *Renunciation of St Francis* (f. 149r.) an attempt is made to suggest the Umbrian topography described in Dante's text. But in the *Meeting with Piccarda and Costanza* (f. 133r.) the landscape is shallow and remote. In a few scenes the intention is locative; the city from which Dante is expelled is identified by its Cathedral as Florence and the city at which he arrives is a construct of Verona. But the towns referred to by Cunizza da Romano and the town and villages described by Cacciaguida are symbols and nothing more. What is portrayed, as any visitor to the Senese will discover for himself, is the Tuscan countryside south of Siena with its sparse trees and rolling hills of which the painter had constant and direct experience.

The third unifying factor is the presence in most of the illuminations of the paired figures of Dante and Beatrice. The subject of the *Paradiso* is a human as well as a mystical experience. Many sophisticated readers regard the figure of Beatrice as a literary device, but at the time this codex was illuminated her existence and physical identity were not open to

doubt. Readers and auditors in the Quattrocento would have been cognisant of the accounts of Beatrice in the *Vita Nuova* and in the life of Dante written by Boccaccio. Boccaccio describes their meeting at a party where Dante as a boy encountered Beatrice as a child of eight. She was, Boccaccio tells us,

> right comely according to her childhood, and full gentle and winning in her ways, and of manners and speech far more sedate and modest than her small age required; and beside this the features of her face [were] full delicate, most excellently disposed, and replete not only with beauty but with virtuous winsomeness, that she was held by many to be a kind of little angel. She then, such as I am painting her, or maybe far more beautious yet, appeared to the eyes of our Dante, at this festival, not I suppose for the first time, but for the first time with power to enamour him; and he, child as he still was, received her fair visage in his heart with such affection, that, from that day forth, never, so long as he lived, did he depart therefrom. . . . As everyone may plainly see, there is naught enduring in this world; and if there be a thing lightly affected with change, that thing is our human life. . . . Of this universal law Dante must learn the weight by another's death sooner than by his own. The most fair Beatrice was well-nigh at the end of her twenty-fourth year, when, as pleased Him who hath all power, she left the anguish of this world and went her way to that glory which her deserts had prepared for her. At which departure Dante was left in such a grief, such affliction, such tears, that many of those nearest him, whether relatives or friends, looked for them to have no other end but only death; and this they thought must briefly come, seeing that he would give no ear to comfort or consolation that was offered him.

Dante's worship of Beatrice, and the growth of the relationship between them is fundamental to the *Paradiso*. Initially didactic – 'Your belief is plunged deep in error,' says Beatrice in the third Canto, 'Do not wonder that I smile at your childish thought' – the association rapidly develops into love. In Canto IV Beatrice looks at Dante 'with eyes so full of the sparkling of love and so divine that my power, vanquished, took flight, and I almost lost myself with eyes downcast.' By Canto XVIII 'I turned round at the loving sound of my comfort, and what love I then saw in the holy eyes I leave here untold.' Ten Cantos later Beatrice ''m 'imparadisa la mente'. With Beatrice's disappearance in Canto XXX the story reaches its celebrated climax: 'From the first day when in this life I saw her face, until this sight the continuing of my song has not been cut off, but now my pursuit must desist from following her beauty further in my verses, as at his utmost reach must every artist.' In the miniatures the figure of Beatrice lights up every scene where she appears. Changes in facial expression could hardly be represented on so small a scale, and the artist's recourse is to posture and proximity. In the earlier Cantos Beatrice and Dante are spaced apart, but slowly they coalesce, and from Canto XVII on Beatrice repeatedly touches Dante with a delicacy that seems, in the context of the artist's use of gesture, to denote love.

All imaginative illustrators live through and in the text that they are illustrating. With Giovanni di Paolo, as we might expect, the spell cast by the *Paradiso* continued long after the present Codex was complete. The earliest example of its influence occurs in 1445 in the panels of the *Creation of the World* and *Paradise* from the Guelfi predella in New York, and

39 the latest appears shortly before 1470 in a complete predella of the *Last Judgment* in the Pinacoteca Nazionale at Siena, where the middle and right hand side as well as the Paradise are based on the *Divine Comedy*. In the centre is a planetary symbol, not unlike that in the New York *Creation of the World*, with a gold centre replacing the mappamondo and its outer edge rotated by seraphim with upturned wings. In the centre sits the Suffering Christ with right arm raised in judgment, and beneath him are the four angels of the Last Judgment and kneeling figures of the Virgin and St John. At either side are the Apostles, two of whom look down in horror at the Hell to which the sinful are consigned. The figures in the *Paradise* are clothed, but two newly risen men are greeted by angels and directed, despite their nakedness, to join the company. Next to them a risen woman without an invitation is forcibly prevented by an angel from gate-crashing Paradise. The dresses of the female figures are less courtly than in the earlier scene, but the two nuns, seemingly Piccarda and Costanza, appear once more. The late *Paradise* is less joyful than the earlier scene; the colour is pallid, the forms are elongated, and the gamut of emotion in the heads is more complex and more self-analytical. But without knowledge of the *Paradiso* it would never have assumed its present form.

The prime function of book illustration is to stimulate the visual faculty and help people to read books. The miniatures reproduced in the present volume are artistically rewarding in themselves, but they will not fulfil their purpose unless they induce those who look at them to follow Dante's journey and embark upon a reading of the poem of which they are the visual counterpart.

Bibliographical Note

In 1929 T.S. Eliot, in his essay on Dante, wrote: 'I do not feel called upon to give any bibliography. Anyone can easily discover more Dante bibliography than anyone can use.' As I myself published in 1947 an annotated survey of the Yates-Thompson Codex of the *Divine Comedy* (*A Sienese Codex of the Divine Comedy*, Oxford and London, 1947), I have desisted from further annotation throughout the present book. The manuscript was described for the first time by Yates-Thompson and Okey (*A Descriptive Catalogue of Fourteen Illuminated Manuscripts Nos. XCV to CVII and 79A completing the Hundred in the Library of Henry Yates-Thompson*, Cambridge, 1912). It was later discussed, in the context of the Aragonese library at Naples, by T. De Marinis (*La biblioteca napoletana dei Re d'Aragona*, 4 vols., Milan, 1947–1953) and, in the broader context of Dante illustration, by P. Brieger, M. Meiss, and C.S. Singleton (*Illuminated Manuscripts of the Divine Comedy*, 2 vols. Princeton, 1969). Fundamental as it is, I have sometimes found myself in disagreement with this invaluable book. The illustrations to the *Paradiso* in the Yates-Thompson Codex have also been carefully discussed in a dissertation by K.A. Wormhoudt (*Manuscript Illuminations by Giovanni di Paolo*, University of Iowa, 1984, issued by University Microfilms International, Ann Arbor, 1992). The best modern account of Giovanni di Paolo's work is that of Carl Straehlke (in *Painting in Renaissance Siena*, New York, 1989, pp. 168–242). His special relationship to Dante was first discussed in an excellent article by P. Rossi ('L'inspirazione dantesca in una pittura di Giovanni di Paolo,' in *Rassegna d'Arte Senese*, xiv, 1921, pp. 138–149).

Photographic acknowledgments

The colour photographs of the Yates-Thompson manuscript were taken by
Laurence Pordes for the British Library. Every miniature is reproduced in
facsimile, often with additional enlarged details; the reproductions of
complete folios on pages 38, 39 and 40 are reduced by about half.

Black-and-white photographs, apart from those supplied by galleries and
museums, are from the following sources:
Alinari 16, 28, 29; Alinari-Anderson 26; Lensini, Siena 24, 38; Mansell
Collection 37; Otto Fein, London 8; Soprintendenza per i Beni Artistici e
Storici, Siena 11, 12, 15, 18, 25, 39.

THE ILLUMINATIONS

by Giovanni di Paolo

Dante prepares to enter the circles of Paradise. He invokes Apollo, the god of poetry, to make him worthy of his task.

On the summit of Parnassus, identified by its two peaks, Dante seeks inspiration from the God of Poetry, Apollo, who proffers him two laurel wreaths. The poet begs Apollo to enter his breast, as he did when flaying the flute-playing satyr Marsyas. Beside Apollo is the laurel tree into which Daphne was transformed when he pursued her, and to its right is the body of Marsyas. On the right a naked orange figure (sometimes interpreted as Pan and sometimes as the living Marsyas) is shown playing a flute.

Beatrice explains to Dante that the universe is a hierarchy, with creatures of different degrees of awareness and capacity all obeying the same divine laws as far as they can perceive them.

Beatrice, who appears for the first time, hovering in the air with Dante, explains the great sea of being, inhabited by creatures outside reason. Dante compares the change effected in himself, when he first caught sight of Beatrice, to the transformation of Glaucus from a land to a sea creature. Above Glaucus is a planetary symbol of the four moral and three theological virtues. Another in the centre shows the heavenly spheres as nine concentric circles ruled by the winged figure of Love.

Dante and Beatrice rise towards the Heaven of the Moon, the first stage of their journey.

Propelled by Minerva and accompanied by Apollo, Dante embarks upon his journey. Above, nine muses point to the Golden Bear. His readers, says Dante, will be even more amazed at what he has to tell than were the Argonauts when, on Colchis, they saw Jason ploughing with two wild bulls. On the right Dante and Beatrice fly up towards the Heaven of the Moon, which is lighted on the left and shaded on the right.

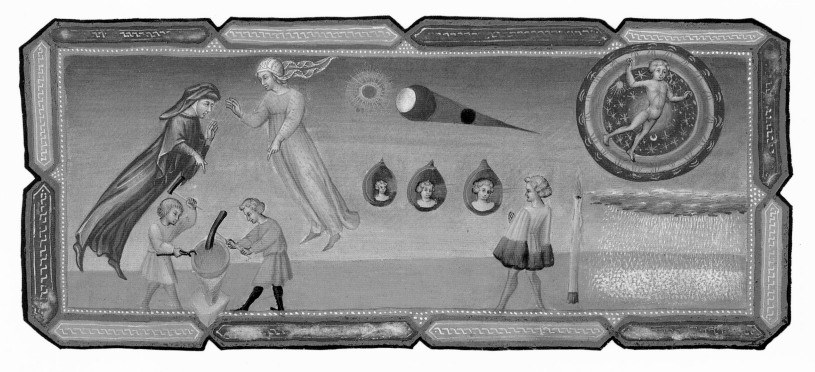

The narrative is interrupted while Beatrice explains to Dante the appearance of the Moon.

In response to Dante's enquiry as to the dark patches on the moon, Beatrice compares the intelligence that controls the planets to a coppersmith (left) working at an anvil. The markings on the surface of the moon are not due to the density of its material but to the shadow it casts upon the earth. This is the subject of a diagram in the centre of the scene. If Dante inspects his own reflection in three mirrors placed at varying distances illuminated by a light behind him, the third image will prove to be as bright as the first two. On the extreme right is the same cosmic symbol as on f.130, with, beneath it, a field of snow.

In the Heaven of the Moon Dante converses with Piccarda dei' Donati and the Empress Costanza.

Dante, with the Sun of love burning on his chest, encounters many shadowy faces, like those reflected in a mirror (left), or in water (right). In the parti-coloured crescent Moon are two Poor Clares, Piccarda de' Donati and the future Empress Costanza, who involuntarily broke their vows, and thus occupy a lowly place in heaven. They are, however, no less happy than its more elevated occupants.

The stories of Piccarda and Costanza. Both were forced to leave their convents because of the political ambitions of their families.

The left half of the scene is occupied with the stories of Piccarda and Costanza. At the back Piccarda, in the white dress of a postulant, enters her convent. In the foreground the two women are wrested from their communities, Piccarda by her brother, Corso de' Donati, and Costanza by the Emperor's son, Conrad. On the right, in a scene that does not occur in the *Paradiso* but is mentioned by one of its commentators: the grandson of the Emperor Henry VI, Conrad, with the arms of Aragon at his feet, pulls down the walls of Naples.

Dante raises questions about moral principles which Beatrice answers partly by drawing on examples from the Scriptures and classical history.

Beatrice realises that Dante is troubled by questions he is unable to express. She compares herself to Daniel interpreting the inexplicable dream of Nebuchadnezzar. In the centre is the king asleep, watched over by Daniel. Above him is the subject of his dream, a figure with golden head, silver arm, belly and thighs of brass, legs of iron, and feet part iron and part clay. Why, Dante enquires of Beatrice, should involuntary actions cause the soul to be consigned to a low place in Paradise? Piccarda and Costanza, replies Beatrice, are as blessed in their places as Moses, Samuel or John the Baptist (seen in a celestial symbol in the upper right corner) are in theirs. The limitation of the human mind requires that figures like the three Archangels (in the foreground on the right) be portrayed in recognisably material fashion.

Beatrice continues her answers to Dante's unspoken questions.

The illustration deals, by analogy, with strength of will. The left hand scene illustrates Plato's belief that the soul, on death, returns to its own star. In the centre are two examples of strength of will, represented by St Lawrence on his grille and Mucius Scaevola placing his hand in a flame. On the right Alcmaeon slays his elderly mother in fulfilment of a vow made to his father.

Beatrice, continuing her discourse on the will, explains the sacred nature of vows and their binding force.

The lessons that Dante has been learning, says Beatrice, are hard and need to be digested, just as, after a heavy meal, men need to sit for a while at table (far left). Vows made to God can be commuted only by God acting through the mediation of St Peter, to whom the keys of absolution have been given. On the right are examples of two vows, the fulfilment of which entailed committing sins worse than the breaking of the vow would have been. The first is Jephtha stabbing his daughter, and the second Agamemnon, who vowed to sacrifice his daughter, Iphigenia, in return for a favourable wind to Troy.

85

Dante and Beatrice leave the Moon and ascend towards the Heaven of Mercury.

The planet is represented as a golden disc, in which the god Mercury, a naked youth, stands surrounded by seven heavenly intelligences. Human beings, here represented by four standing youths, Beatrice insists have guides to salvation in the Old and New Testaments and the voice of the Church (represented by a Pope, holding the two open books). A thousand splendours draw round them eagerly, just as fish in a pond rise in expectation of being fed.

In the Heaven of Mercury Dante encounters the Emperor Justinian, who gives him a condensed account of the history of the Roman Empire.

The sphere of Mercury is here occupied by Justinian, and the scenes below illustrate his narrative. First Aeneas carries the imperial standard through the gates of Rome, identified by the Pyramid of Cestius. Next, Constantine carries the same standard through the gates of Constantinople, the 'Second Rome', but Christian, not pagan. Lastly, Justinian himself kneels before Agapetus, a 6th-century pope who – according to the history current in Dante's time – converted him from the Monophysite heresy to belief in the dual nature of Christ.

Justinian, going on to a period of history later than his own, tells the story of Romeo, a 13th-century minister of Raymond Berengar IV, Count of Provence.

In the planetary circle Justinian is now replaced by Romeo, who had been responsible for arranging the marriages of Raymond's four daughters to Louis IX of France, Henry III of England, the Earl of Cornwall and Charles of Anjou. The queens are shown seated on a bench, with, to the right, their husbands, two of them identified by the arms on their shields. Despite his services, Romeo was disgraced through the jealousy of the Provençal lords, ending his life in poverty. He is here dressed as a beggar.

Beatrice explains to Dante the mystery of the Redemption, by which the sin of Adam and Eve was wiped away by God becoming man and suffering punishment in His own person.

The figure of Justinian kneeling in prayer returns to the planetary circle. On the right are the three crucial events in the redemption of mankind: the Fall, the Annunciation and the Crucifixion.

93

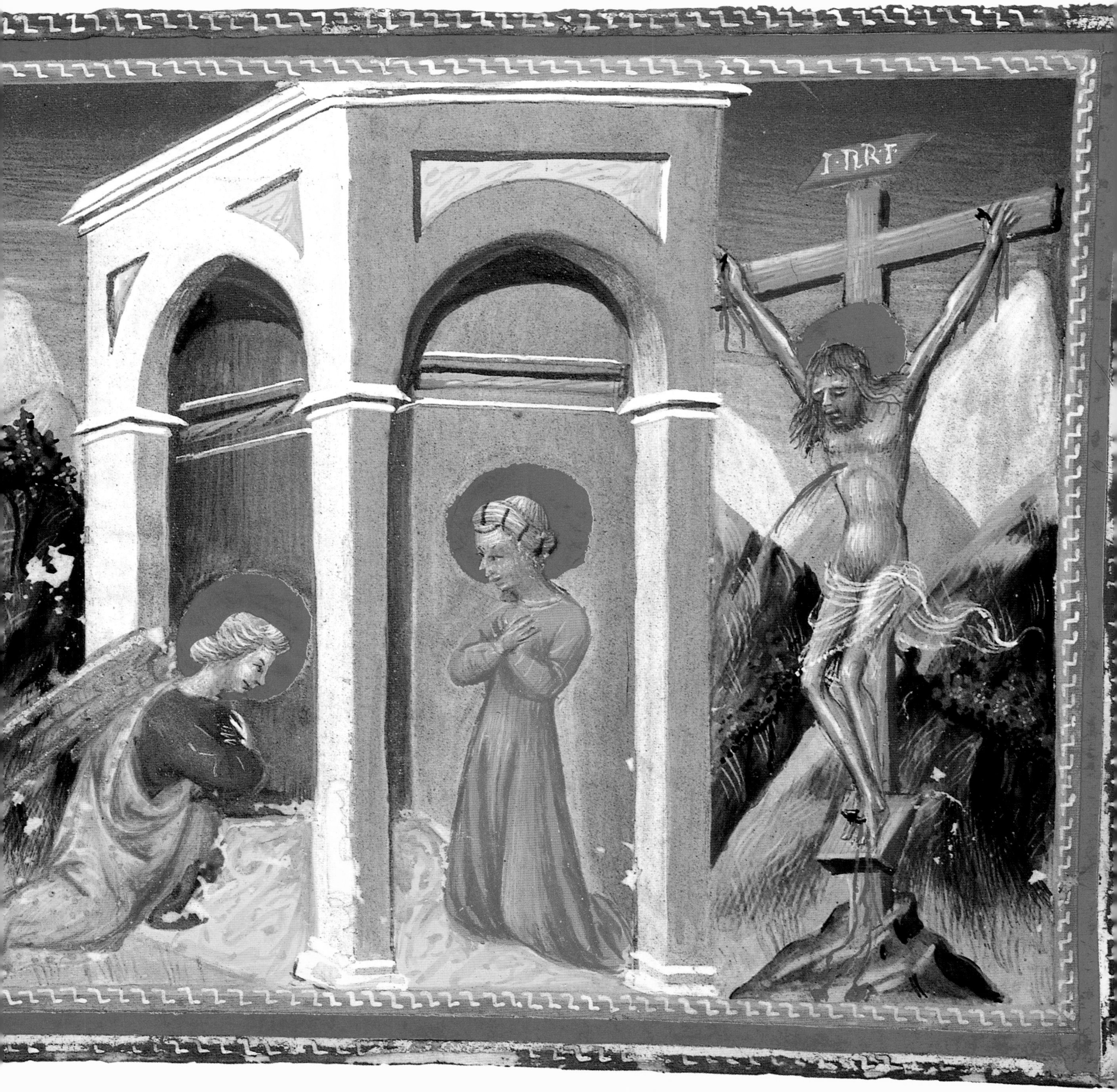
I·NRI

Dante and Beatrice rise from the Heaven of Mercury to that of Venus.

On the island of Cyprus stands the temple of Venus, whom men in antiquity worshipped 'in their ancient error'. Venus is accompanied by two children, who owe their presence to a passage in a fourteenth-century commentary in which Venus is said to have had two sons, Cupid and Amor.

97

*Dante questions the souls of those in the Heaven of Venus, beginning with
Charles Martel.*

In the planetary circle stands Charles Martel (born 1271), who tells Dante
that his descendants would still be ruling Sicily had it not been for the
rebellion known as the Sicilian Vespers (1282) when the house of Anjou
lost the island to that of Aragon. The shields carried by the invading
soldiers bear the Aragonese arms. Mount Etna appears in the background
on the right.

Still in the Heaven of Venus, Dante speaks to Cunizza da Romano, the sister of the ferocious tyrant Ezzelino da Romano.

Cunizza addresses Dante from the circle of Venus. In Dante's childhood Cunizza, after an eventful life that included four husbands and many lovers, was living quietly in Florence occupied in charitable deeds. Beneath her are represented the valleys of the Brenta and the Po and the cities of Padua, Treviso, Feltre and Ferrara.

Dante talks to Folco of Marseilles who deplores the avarice of the Church.

The figure of Folco, dressed in a Cistercian habit and holding a crozier, joins that of Cunizza in the circle of Venus. A troubadour poet of love, he later became a monk and died as Bishop of Toulouse. He condemns especially the city of Florence, the offspring of the devil and the producer of 'that cursed flower', the florin, the cause of corruption in the Church. Giovanni di Paolo shows the devil pouring gold from a money-bag into the hands of a pope. Florence is represented by its cathedral (its octagonal dome is finished but it still lacks its crowning lantern) and its campanile. The two gateways bear the symbol of the Florentine lily.

Dante and Beatrice leave the Heaven of Venus and approach that of the Sun.

The Sun is a wheel of green, white and gold circles, from which golden rays descend over a panorama of hills and castellated farms.

In the Heaven of the Sun, Dante and Beatrice meet those distinguished for their wisdom.

Amid the golden rays of the Sun, Dante is greeted by St Thomas Aquinas with Albertus Magnus at his side. Below are seated ten representatives of wisdom, who include the Venerable Bede, St Ambrose, Isidore of Seville, Dionysius the Aeropagite, Solomon, Boethius, Gratian, Peter Lombard, Richard of St Victor and Siger of Brabant.

Still in the Heaven of the Sun, St Thomas Aquinas presents Dante to St Dominic and St Francis, the founders of the two great mendicant orders.

Within an aureole of golden light, St Thomas gestures towards St Dominic and St Francis (wearing, respectively, Dominican and Franciscan habits), both standing on winged cherubim.

St Thomas Aquinas tells Dante the story of St Francis stripping himself of all his possessions and dedicating himself to poverty.

The naked figure of St Francis, vowed to poverty, receives the benediction of the Bishop of Assisi. The Umbrian landscape, with Assisi on the left and Gubbio on the right, is that described by Dante.

St Bonaventure tells Dante the story of St Dominic and his mission to the heathen.

St Bonaventure, in Franciscan habit, occupies the circle of the Sun. On the right St Dominic, in front of a walled town by a seashore (Calaroga, in Spain), preaches to a group of heathens.

St Bonaventure continues his discourse and introduces a further circle of learned men.

Bonaventure introduces a semi-circle of saints, scholars and prophets. In the centre is St Thomas Aquinas holding an open volume of the *Summa*. The other figures include two early followers of St Francis, Fra Agostino and Illuminato da Rieti, Hugh of St Victor, Peter Comestor, Peter of Spain (Pope John XXI), St John Chrysostom, and other 'sapienti'.

Dante describes the lights of Heaven revolving round him and Beatrice like stars, and makes an allusion to the Corona Borealis, or Ariadne's Crown.

On the left is Theseus slaying the Minotaur on the island of Crete. On the right, on the island of Naxos, the abandoned Ariadne is roused by a figure of Amor.

St Thomas Aquinas discourses on the nature of God's gift of wisdom to Solomon.

Beneath a radiant Sun – itself the symbol of God's wisdom – sits Christ between Adam and Solomon. To the left is Adam, the perfect being created from earth by God's essence. In the centre is Christ, the product of a divine act of a higher order. To the right is Solomon, the channel for the word of God.

Beatrice questions the souls in the Heaven of the Sun concerning the nature of the risen body after the Last Judgment and the degree of radiance that they will generate. Solomon answers her.

The gold rays of the sun illuminate a crowd of naked bodies newly risen from their tombs.

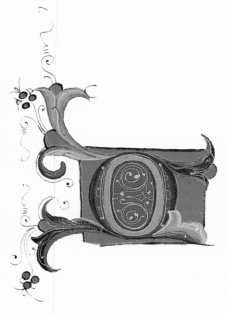

Dante and Beatrice rise from the Heaven of the Sun to that of Mars. One of the souls there comes speeding towards them. He proves to be an ancestor of Dante's, Cacciaguida, who had served in the Second Crusade and died in battle in 1147.

Cacciaguida, wearing the Crusader's cross, points with his right hand to the figure of Aeneas. Below on the right Aeneas (dressed as he was in f.139r. and bearing the same arms on his shield) is seen greeting his father Anchises in the Elysian fields. In the lower left corner is a sleeping male nude and a naked female figure whose presence is unexplained.

Cacciaguida tells the story of his life, how he was knighted by the Emperor Conrad III and fell in battle.

On the left Cacciaguida is girded by the Emperor Conrad with a scarlet sword. In the centre he leaves on horseback for the Crusade, and on the right he is slain by a Saracen.

Cacciaguida turns from his narrative to speak of the families of 12th-century Florence and to criticize the vices that corrupt them.

Cacciaguida laments the influx of families from the countryside into the city of Florence. The townships which he mentions, some of which may be portrayed in the miniature, include Certaldo, Fogline, Galuzzo and Trespiano.

Dante asks his ancestor to foretell his own fate. Cacciaguida warns him that he will be exiled from Florence as Hippolytus was exiled from Athens.

Dante, when accompanied by Virgil through Hell and Purgatory, had heard 'heavy words' about his future life. These are confirmed by Cacciaguida, who predicts that he will be exiled as Hippolytus was exiled from Athens, leaving everything he loved most dearly. The woman seated on the left is Phaedra, the stepmother of Hippolytus. In the centre Hippolytus reluctantly leaves Athens and on the right the horses of his chariot bolt and drag him to his death.

Dante was banished from Florence in March 1302, and this scene is devoted to his exile.

On the left he is thrust out of the gate of Florence, which bears the sign of the lily. The Duomo is portrayed as in f.145r., without Brunelleschi's lantern. On the right is the city of Verona where Dante sought refuge with Can Grande della Scala. He is shown in a loggia overlooking the river Adige, writing his great poem.

Still in the Heaven of Mars, Dante is shown eight holy warriors who appear in the form of a cross.

The circle is filled with the winged figure of Mars. From it protrude the head and shoulders of Cacciaguida. The cross is made up of eight warrior heroes drawn from a variety of sources – the Old Testament (Joshua, holding the Sun which he bade stand still, and Judas Maccabaeus), history (Charlemagne, Godefroi de Bouillon and Robert Guiscard) and medieval romance (Roland; William, Count of Orange; and Reynard).

Dante and Beatrice leave the Heaven of Mars and enter that of Jupiter. Here the souls are like lights who arrange themselves as letters to spell out the sentence from The Book of Wisdom, *'Love Justice, ye who judge the earth.'*

Jupiter stands within the circle. To the right, in a 'round flock', are the souls of the just rulers which, in Dante's text, but not in this illumination, make up the letter M of TERRAM and are then mutated into the form of an eagle. In the present scene only the head and neck of the eagle have manifested themselves.

The eagle is now fully formed with wings outspread. For Dante it symbolized both divine justice and imperial authority.

The eagle is here fully formed. Through its beak, the souls of which it is composed with one voice answer Dante's questions concerning justice.

Dante questions the eagle on the subject of divine justice. The eagle, in reply,
denounces a number of unjust rulers.

Giovanni di Paolo shows ten of the crowned heads who are condemned
by the eagle: Albert of Austria, Philip IV of France, Edward I of
England, Ferdinand IV of Castile, Wenceslaus IV of Bohemia, Charles
II of Naples, Frederick of Sicily, James of Majorca, James of Aragon and
Diniz of Portugal. Above them is the Book of Judgment.

The eagle turns from the unjust to the just rulers, and bids Dante look at the souls who make up its eye and eyebrow. In the eye he sees the figure of King David.

On the head and wings of the eagle stand (left to right) Trajan, Hezekiah, Constantine and William II of Sicily. The eye of the eagle is filled by David.

Dante and Beatrice enter the Heaven of Saturn. Beatrice's beauty glows brighter as they ascend, and she warns Dante that if she were to smile he would, like Semele, be destroyed by its radiance.

Saturn is represented as an old man with a sickle. A ladder beneath the heavenly sphere is held in place by four angels. In the lower left corner lies the burning body of Semele, who asked to see her lover Jupiter in his full splendour and was reduced to ashes.

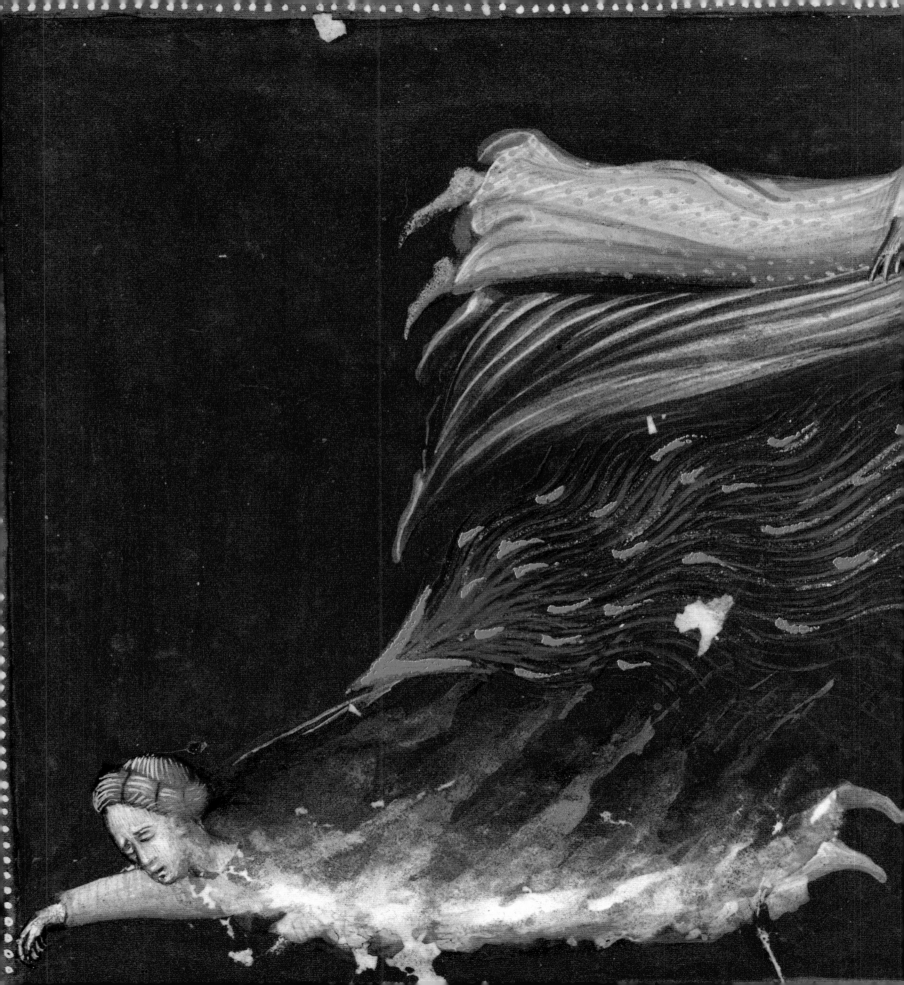

Although placed on a page with the text of Canto XXI, this miniature refers back to Canto XX, where the eagle addresses Dante and speaks of recent rulers in Italy. The wise rule of William II is praised and contrasted with that of his successors, Charles II and Frederick of Aragon.

The figures are rulers of Sicily, Robert Guiscard, William II, Charles II, Frederick of Aragon.

In the Heaven of Saturn, Dante and Beatrice meet St Peter Damian, who speaks of his own life and search for holiness.

In the sky Peter Damian is dressed in a Benedictine habit with a scarlet cardinal's hat. To the right he is seen twice more – reading in a cave and seated outside a monastery. The rocky landscape is that of the Benedictine monastery of Fonte Avellana on the slopes of Monte Catria.

The next soul to address Dante and Beatrice is that of St Benedict, the founder of the Benedictine Order.

St Benedict is shown in a Benedictine habit wearing the pallium. On the right he is shown assaulting a marble shrine containing a golden figure of the god Apollo, thus reclaiming the peasants near his monastery from superstition and 'impious worship'. On the extreme right is a Benedictine monastery, possibly Monte Cassino.

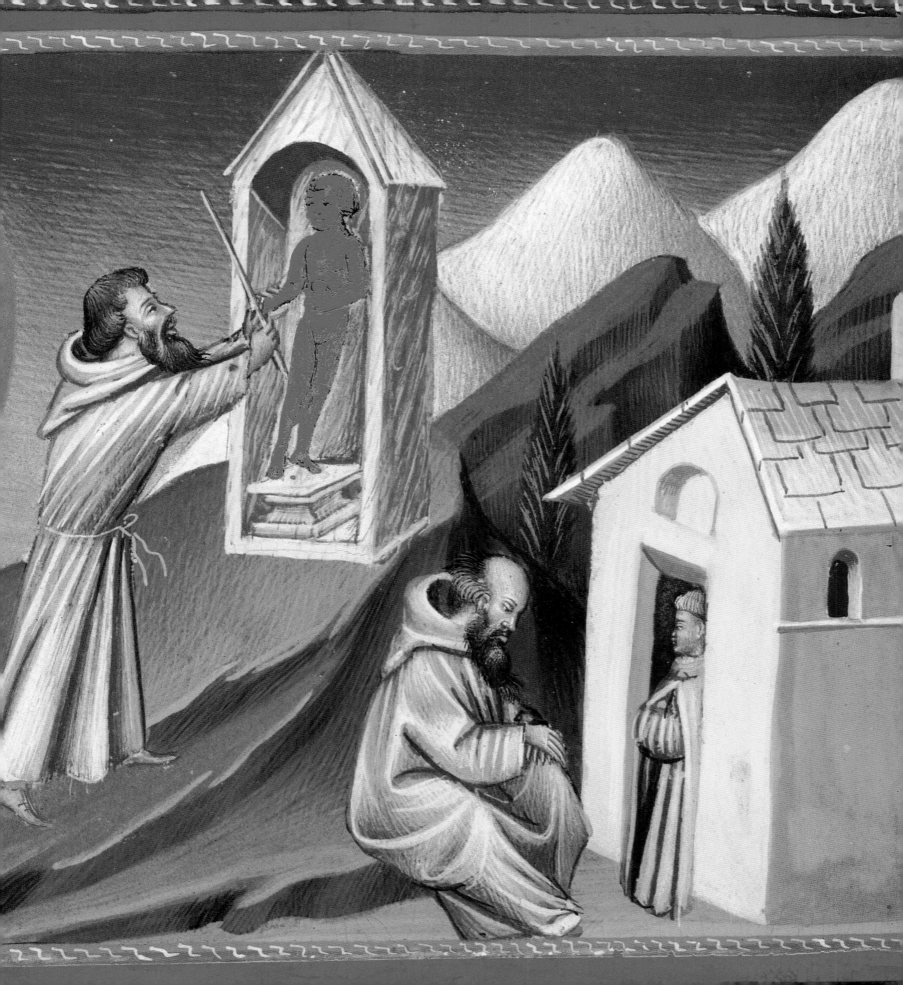

Dante and Beatrice rise to the Heaven of the Fixed Stars, and can look back at all the seven planets beneath them.

The figure in the centre is Leda holding her twins, Castor and Pollux, the constellation of Gemini. Below on the left is the Sun, a scarlet figure in a flaming chariot, and on the right the Moon, Mars, Mercury, Jupiter, Venus and Saturn. The figures are arranged not in the sequence in which they appear in the *Paradiso*, but in the order of the days of the week.

Dante and Beatrice now approach the zenith and for the first time can see the radiance of Christ himself.

Christ leans out from a circle of six-pointed stars. Beneath, 'the hosts of Christ's triumph', kneeling in worship, bathe in the radiance that streams from Him.

With strengthened vision, Dante can now see the Virgin herself, surrounded by a host of angels.

In a mandorla of angels is Christ, holding the Old and New Testaments. Beneath him is St Peter, holding a key in either hand, and the Virgin Mary.

In the Heaven of the Fixed Stars, St Peter interrogates Dante on his Christian Faith.

From a circle of stars St Peter, with two keys in his left hand and his right hand raised, addresses Dante and Beatrice.

At the end of his catechism, St Peter girds Dante three times as a blessing.

St Peter leans forward to encircle Dante with a thin white cord. On the right, bearing a cross, is the crowned figure of Faith, and behind St Peter stands a group of blessed souls.

St James and St John now appear to Dante and question him on two other cardinal virtues, Hope and Charity.

The two sides of this miniature represent the two separate episodes. On the left the kneeling Dante is questioned by St James, who is represented twice, within the circle and as a head protruding from it. To the left is the flying figure of Hope. On the right is St John the Evangelist with the figure of Charity. The upper half of the circle shows the suffering and triumphant Christ.

St John, now represented in old age, questions Dante on the subject of charity. At the end of his answer Dante's sight is restored to him.

St John faces to the left with, behind him, six souls kneeling in adoration.

The soul of Adam appears and tells Dante about the story of the Fall.

Adam is depicted as the youth of the temptation, not as the venerable
figure released from limbo. Five other souls who follow him are
unidentified. On the left is the Mount of Paradise, with the four rivers
flowing from it.

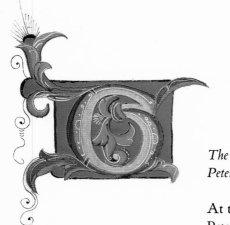

The heavenly host glorifies the Trinity, adored by three kneeling figures, while St Peter continues his discourse by condemning the vices of his successors.

At the top of the circle are the three Persons of the Trinity. On the left St Peter gestures with his key to the seated figure of a pope. It was never his intention, says St Peter, that the symbol of the keys should figure on the banner of a soldier fighting against the baptized (symbolised by the two men in armour in front of him and the casque behind), nor that his signet should seal corrupt privileges (symbolised by the papal bull on the right). The animal beside the pope is a rapacious wolf mentioned in Dante's text.

Dante and Beatrice ascend to the ninth Heaven of Paradise, the Primum Mobile.

Giovanni di Paolo represents the Primum Mobile as a ring of golden light, framed by Cherubim and containing a reduced *mappamondo*, which shows the point in his journey that Dante has reached. In the centre is the commanding figure of Christ the Redeemer.

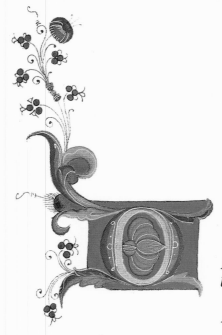

Dante is able to look directly at the light of God, which he sees as an infinitely bright point surrounded by rings which Beatrice identifies as the orders of angels.

At the centre of the sphere is the head of the wind god, Boreas.

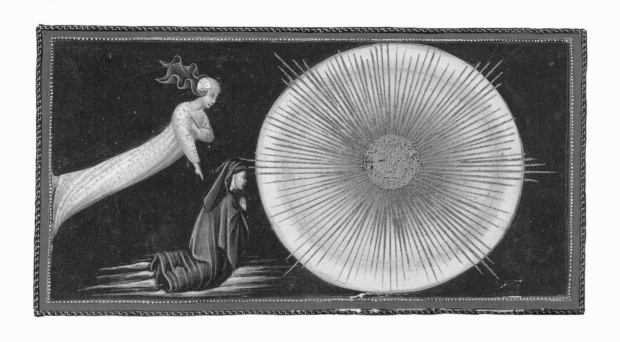

Beatrice explains the relationship between the Heavens and the orders of angels.

Beneath another representation of the Trinity, surrounded by the wings of
the seraphim, kneels a host of angels, divided into three hierarchies, dressed
in pink, blue and yellow. On the right sits Dionysius, holding his book
On the Celestial Hierarchy.

*Beatrice continues her explanation of the relationship between the universe
and the angels.*

Beneath the familiar Trinity, Lucifer and the rebel angels, transformed into
devils, are driven down to Hell by the archangels Michael and Raphael.

Beatrice concludes her discourse with a diatribe against modern preachers, who indulge their own fancies instead of preaching orthodox doctrine.

This is the last of Giovanni di Paolo's narrative illustrations. The preacher, a friar, stands at a pulpit facing his congregation, who are unable to see the devil nestling in his hood. The pig was the symbol of St Anthony the Abbot, and the fattened pig held by a farmer on the right is a symbol of greed.

Dante and Beatrice rise to the highest Heaven of all, the Empyrean, represented by a river of light.

Sparks of light (the *faville vive* of Dante's text) rise from the river and drop back into it. Giovanni di Paolo, following Dante, represents these as naked souls swimming and diving in a stream fringed by lilies and reeds.

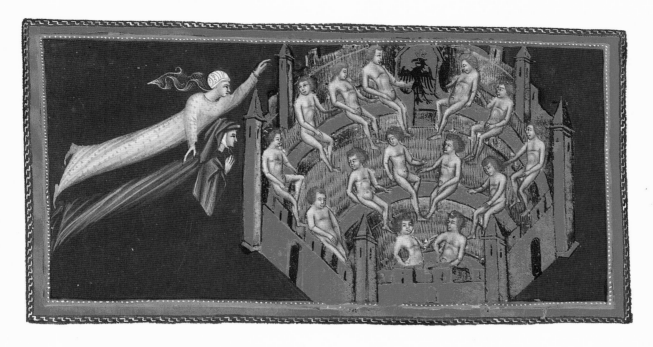

As Beatrice continues her description, the metaphor of the river of light gives way to that of the Celestial Jerusalem, which, for Dante, carried contemporary political associations.

The scene is a tiered amphitheatre within a walled city containing fourteen seated figures. The central seat at the back, bearing the emblem of the imperial eagle, is vacant. This was destined in Dante's mind for the Emperor Henry VII, who, however, died prematurely in 1313. This iconography stems from the belief that the emperor's temporal power was ordained by God.

At this point we reach the image which dominates the closing cantos of the 'Paradiso', the celestial rose.

The miniature illustrates the lines at the beginning of the thirty-first canto: 'In form then of a pure white rose the saintly host was shown to me, which with His own blood Christ made His bride.' Nine angels described by Dante as 'enflowering themselves like a swarm of bees' rest in the petals. The Trinity fill the stamen of the flower.

St Bernard shows Dante, at the edge of the celestial rose, the Virgin in glory.

The Virgin, holding the child, is shown seated in a flower-filled garden. Round her are five angels. On the right kneels St Bernard, Dante's sponsor in the last pages of the poem.

Beatrice shows Dante another vision of the celestial rose.

The central place is occupied by the Virgin and Child. Eve lies beneath the Virgin's feet. To the left is St Peter and to the right St John the Baptist, in a pose reminiscent of the Ecce Agnus Dei, pointing towards the Child. Beneath Eve are representations of St Anne and St Lucy, and in the outer petals are St Francis, St Augustine, St Bernard and a female saint.

Dante asks St Bernard to tell the name of the angel who looks so intently at the Virgin. St Bernard replies that it is Gabriel, the angel of the Annunciation.

The Virgin and Annunciatory Angel occupy the top of the rose. Below is St Anne, the Virgin's mother, and under her Moses with the tablets of the Law. Dante is shown plucking St Bernard by the sleeve.

The last canto opens with St Bernard's famous prayer to the Virgin.

St Bernard is shown addressing the Virgin with the great prayer: 'Virgin Mother, daughter of thy Son, humble and exalted more than any other creature, fixed goal of the eternal counsel, thou art she who did so ennoble human nature that its Maker did not disdain to become its creature. In thy womb was rekindled the love whose warmth this flower in the eternal peace has thus unfolded.'

Dante ends his poem with a vision of divine love which encompasses and contains everything, leaving his mind as dazed as that of Neptune when he saw the shadow of the first boat, Argo, on the sea.

On the left Dante, still accompanied by Beatrice, kneels in adoration before the Virgin of the Assumption. On the right, Neptune, with right arm raised, registers wonder at the sight of Jason's boat, the Argo, sailing across the sea.

PARADISO

Translated by Charles Singleton

Canto I

THE GLORY of the All-Mover penetrates through the universe and reglows in one part more, and in another less. I have been in the heaven that most receives of His light, and have seen things which whoso descends from up there has neither the knowledge nor the power to relate, because, as it draws near to its desire, our intellect enters so deep that memory cannot go back upon the track. Nevertheless, so much of the holy kingdom as I could treasure up in my mind shall now be the matter of my song.

O good Apollo, for this last labor make me such a vessel of your worth as you require for granting your beloved laurel. Thus far the one peak of Parnassus has sufficed me, but now I have need of both, as I enter the arena that remains. Enter into my breast and breathe there as when you drew Marsyas from the sheath of his limbs. O divine Power, if you do so lend yourself to me that I may show forth the image of the blessed realm which is imprinted in my mind, you shall see me come to your beloved tree and crown me with those leaves of which the matter and you shall make me worthy. So rarely, father, are they gathered, for triumph of caesar or of poet — fault and shame of human wills — that the Peneian frond ought to beget gladness in the glad Delphic deity whenever it causes anyone to long for it. A great flame follows a little spark: perhaps, after me, prayer shall be offered with better voices, that Cyrrha may respond.

The lamp of the world rises to mortals through different passages; but through that which joins four circles with three crosses it issues with a better course and conjoined with better stars, and tempers and stamps the wax of the world more after its own fashion. Almost such an outlet had made morning there and evening here, and all the hemisphere there was white, and the other dark, when I saw Beatrice turned to her left side and looking at the sun: never did eagle so fix his gaze thereon. And even as a second ray is wont to issue from the first, and mount upwards again, like a pilgrim who would return home: thus of her action, infused through the eyes into my imagination, mine was made, and I fixed my eyes on the sun beyond our wont. Much is granted to our faculties there that is not granted here, by virtue of the place made for humankind as its proper abode. I did not endure it long, nor so little that I did not see it sparkle round about, like iron that comes molten from the fire. And suddenly day seemed added to day, as if He who has the power had adorned heaven with another sun.

Beatrice was standing with her eyes all fixed upon the eternal wheels, and I fixed mine on her, withdrawn from there above. Gazing upon her I became within me such as Glaucus became on tasting of the grass that made him sea-fellow of the other gods. The passing beyond humanity may not be set forth in words: therefore let the example suffice any for whom grace reserves that experience.

Whether I was but that part of me which Thou didst create last, O Love that rulest the heavens, Thou knowest, who with Thy light didst lift me. When the revolution which Thou, by being desired, makest eternal turned my attention unto itself by the harmony which Thou dost temper and distinguish, so much of the heaven seemed to me then to be kindled by the sun's flame that rain or river never made a lake so wide. The novelty of the sound and the great light kindled in me a desire to know their cause, never before felt with such keenness. Whereupon she who saw me as I saw myself, to quiet my perturbed mind, opened her lips before I opened mine to ask, and began, 'You make yourself dull with false imagining, so that you do not see what you would see had you cast it off. You are not on earth as you believe; but lightning, fleeing its proper site, never darted so fast as you are returning to yours.'

If by these brief words which she smiled to me I was freed from my first perplexity, within a new one I became the more enmeshed; and I said, 'I was already content concerning one great wonder; but now I marvel how it can be that I should pass through these light bodies.'

Whereupon, after a pitying sigh, she turned her eyes on me with the look that a mother casts on her delirious child. And she began, 'All things have order among themselves, and this is the form that makes the universe like God. Herein the high creatures behold the imprint of the Eternal Worth, which is the end wherefor the aforesaid ordinance is made. In the order whereof I speak all natures are inclined by different lots, nearer and less near unto their principle; wherefore they move to different ports over the great sea of being, each with an instinct given it to bear it on: this bears fire upward toward the moon; this is the motive force in mortal creatures; this binds together and unites the earth. And not only does this bow shoot these creatures that lack intelligence, but also those that have intellect and love. The Providence which ordains all this, with Its light makes ever quiet that heaven within which revolves the sphere that has the greatest speed; and thither now, as to a place decreed, the virtue of that bow-string bears us on, which aims at a joyful target whatsoever it shoots.

'To be sure, even as a shape often does not accord with the intention of the art, because the material is deaf to respond, so the creature sometimes departs from this course, having the power, thus impelled, to swerve toward some other part; and even as the fire from a cloud may be seen to fall downwards, so the primal impulse, diverted by false pleasure, is turned toward earth. You should not wonder more at your rising, if I deem aright, than at a stream that falls from a mountain top to the base. It would be a marvel if you, being freed from hindrance, had settled down below, even as stillness would be in living fire on earth.'

Then she turned her gaze heavenwards again.

Canto II

O YOU that are in your little bark, eager to hear, following behind my ship that singing makes her way, turn back to see again your shores. Do not commit yourselves to the open sea, for perchance, if you lost me, you would remain astray. The water which I take was never coursed before. Minerva breathes and Apollo guides me, and nine Muses point out to me the Bears.

You other few who lifted up your necks betimes for bread of angels, on which men here subsist but never become sated of it, you may indeed commit your vessel to the deep brine, holding to my furrow ahead of the water that turns smooth again. Those glorious ones who crossed the sea to Colchis, when they saw Jason turned plowman, were not as amazed as you shall be.

The inborn and perpetual thirst for the deiform realm bore us away, swift almost as you see the heavens. Beatrice was gazing upward, and I on her; and perhaps in that time that a bolt strikes, flies, and from the catch is released, I saw myself arrived where a wondrous thing drew my sight to it. She, therefore, from whom my thoughts could not be hidden, turned toward me, as glad as she was fair, and 'Direct your mind to God in gratitude,' she said, 'who has united us with the first star.'

It seemed to me that a cloud had enveloped us, shining, dense, solid and polished, like a diamond smitten by the sun. Within itself the eternal pearl received us, as water receives a ray of light, itself remaining uncleft. If I was body (and if here we conceive not how one bulk could brook another, which must be if body enters body), the more should longing enkindle us to see that Essence wherein we behold how our nature and God united themselves. There that which we hold by faith shall be seen, not demonstrated, but known of itself, like the first truth that man believes.

I answered, 'My Lady, devoutly as I most may, I do thank Him who has removed me from the mortal world. But tell me, what are the dusky marks of this body which there below on earth cause folk to tell the tale of Cain?'

She smiled a little, and then said to me, 'If the judgment of mortals errs where the key of sense does not unlock, truly the shafts of wonder should not prick you henceforth, since even when following after the senses you see that reason's wings are short. But tell me what you yourself think of it.'

And I, 'That which appears to us diverse here above I suppose to be produced by rare and dense matter.'

And she, 'Verily you shall see that your belief is plunged deep in error, if you listen well to the argument I shall make against it.

'The eighth sphere displays to you many lights which both in quality and in magnitude can be seen to be of diverse countenances. If rarity and density alone produced this thing, one single virtue, more or less or equally distributed, would be in all. Different virtues must needs be fruits of formal principles, the which, save only one, would be destroyed, according to your reckoning. Further, were rarity the cause of that darkness whereof you make question, either this planet would thus be lacking in its matter quite through and through, or else, just as fat and lean are distributed in a body, it would alternate the pages in its volume. If the first were the case, this would be manifest in the eclipse of the sun, by the shining through of the light, as it does when it is poured upon any rare matter. This is not so; therefore we must look at the other supposition, and if it chance that I quash that, your opinion will be refuted.

'If it be that this rarity does not pass throughout, needs must there be a limit at which its contrary intercepts its passing farther, and thence that other's ray would be cast back, just as color returns from the glass that hides lead behind itself. Now you will say that the ray shows itself dimmer there than in other parts, because it is reflected there from farther back. From this objection experiment, which is wont to be the fountain to the streams of your arts, may deliver you, if ever you try it. You shall take three mirrors, and set two of them equally remote from you, and let the other, even more remote, meet your eyes between the first two. Turning toward them, cause a light to be placed behind your back which may shine in the three mirrors and return to you reflected from all three. Although the more distant image may not reach you so great in quantity, you will there see it must needs be of equal brightness with the others.

'Now — as beneath the blows of the warm rays the substrate of the snow is left stripped both of the color and the coldness which it had — you, left thus stripped in your intellect, will I inform with light so living that it shall quiver as you look on it.

'Within the heaven of the divine peace revolves a body in whose power lies the being of all that it contains. The following heaven, which has so many things to show, distributes this being through diverse essences, distinct from it and contained by it. The other circles, by various differentiatings, dispose the distinctions which they have within themselves unto their ends and their sowings. These organs of the universe proceed, as you now see, from grade to grade, for they receive from above and operate downwards. Observe well now how I advance through this pass to the truth which you seek, so that hereafter you may know how to take the ford alone. The motion and the virtue of the holy spheres, even as the hammer's art by the smith, must needs be inspired by the blessed movers; and the heaven which so many lights make beautiful takes its stamp from the profound mind that turns it, and of that stamp makes itself the seal. And as the soul within your dust is diffused through different members and conformed to different potencies, so does the Intelligence deploy its goodness, multiplied through the stars, itself circling upon its own unity. Divers virtues make divers alloy with the precious body it quickens, wherein, even as life in you, it is bound. Because of the glad nature whence it flows, the mingled virtue shines through the body, as gladness does through a living pupil. Thence comes what seems different between light and light, not from density and rarity. This is the formal principle which produces, conformably with its own excellence, the dark and the bright.'

Canto III

THAT SUN which first had heated my breast with love, proving and refuting, had uncovered to me the sweet aspect of fair truth, and, to confess me corrected and assured, I raised my head more erect to speak, in measure as was meet; but a sight appeared which held me so fast to itself, to look on it, that I bethought me not of my confession.

As though smooth and transparent glass, or through clear and tranquil waters, yet not so deep that the bottom be lost, the outlines of our faces return so faint that a pearl on a white brow comes not less boldly to our eyes, so did I behold many a countenance eager to speak; wherefore I fell into the contrary error to that which kindled love between the man and the fountain. No sooner was I aware of them than, taking them for mirrored faces, I turned round my eyes to see of whom they were, and saw nothing; and I turned them forward again, straight into the light of the sweet guide, whose holy eyes were glowing as she smiled.

'Do not wonder,' she said to me, 'that I smile at your childish thought, since it does not yet trust itself upon the truth, but turns you, after its wont, to vacancy. These that you see are real substances, assigned here for failure in there vows. Wherefore speak with them and hear and believe, for the true light that satisfies them does not suffer them to turn their steps aside from it.'

And I directed myself to the shade who seemed most eager to speak, and I began like a man whom excessive desire confuses, 'O well-created spirit, who in the rays of life eternal do taste the sweetness which, if not tasted, is never understood, it would be a kindness to me if you satisfied me with your name and with your lot.'

Whereon she, eager and with smiling eyes, 'Our charity does not shut the doors against right will any more than that which wills that all Its court be like Itself. In the world I was a virgin sister, and if your memory be searched well, my being more beautiful will not conceal me from you, but you will recognize that I am Piccarda, who, placed here with these other blessèd ones, am blessèd in the slowest sphere. Our affections, which are kindled solely in the pleasure of the Holy Ghost, rejoice in being conformed to His order. And this lot, which appears so lowly, is given to use because our vows were neglected and void in some particular.'

Whereon I said to her, 'In your wondrous aspects a something divine shines forth that transmutes you from recollection of former times; therefore I was not quick in calling you to mind, but now that which you tell me helps me so that I more clearly recall your features. But tell me, you who are happy here, do you desire a more exalted place, to see more, and to make yourselves more dear?'

With those other shades she first smiled a little, then answered me so glad that she seemed to burn in the first fire of love, 'Brother, the power of love quiets our will and makes us wish only for that which we have and gives us no other thirst. Did we desire to be more aloft, our longings would be discordant with His will who assigns us here: which you will see is not possible in these circles if to exist in charity here is of necessity, and if you well consider what is love's nature. Nay, it is the essence of this blessed existence to keep itself within the divine will, whereby our wills themselves are made one; so that our being thus from threshold to threshold throughout this realm is a joy to all the realm as to the King, who draws our wills to what He wills; and in His will is our peace. It is that sea to which all moves, both what It creates and what nature makes.'

Then was it clear to me how everywhere in Heaven is Paradise, even if the grace of the Supreme Good does not there rain down in one same measure. But as it happens when of one food we have enough and the appetite for another still remains, that this is asked for and thanks are returned for that, so I did with gesture and with speech, to learn from her what was the web through which she had not drawn the shuttle to the end.

'Perfect life and high merit enheaven a lady more aloft,' she said to me, 'according to whose rule, in your world below, are those who take the robe and veil themselves that they, even till death, may wake and sleep with that Spouse who accepts every vow which love conforms unto His pleasure. From the world, to follow her, I fled while yet a girl, and in her habit I clothed me and promised myself to the way of her order. Then men, more used to evil than to good, snatched me from the sweet cloister: and God knows what then my life became.

'And this other splendor which shows itself to you at my right side, and which is enkindled with all the light of our sphere, understands of herself that which I say of me. She was a sister, and from her head in like manner was taken the shadow of the sacred veil. Yet, turned back as she was into the world, against her will and against right custom, from her heart's veil she was never loosed. This is the light of the great Constance, who bore to the second blast of Swabia the third and final power.'

Thus did she speak to me, and then began to sing *Ave Maria*, and, singing, vanished, as through deep water some heavy thing. My sight, which followed her so far as was possible, after it lost her, turned to the mark of greater desire and wholly reverted to Beatrice. but she so flashed upon my gaze that at first my sight endured it not; and this made me the slower with my questioning.

Canto IV

BETWEEN TWO foods, distant and appetizing in equal measure, a free man would die of hunger before he would bring one of them to his teeth. So would a lamb stand between two cravings of fierce wolves, in equal fear of both; so would a hound stand still between two hinds. Wherefore, if I was silent, urged in equal measure by my doubts, I neither blame nor commend myself, since it was of necessity.

I was silent, but my desire was depicted on my face, and my questioning with it, in warmer colors far than by distinct speech. Beatrice did what Daniel did, when he lifted Nebuchadnezzar out of the wrath that had made him unjustly cruel, and she said, 'I see well how one and another desire so draw you on that your eagerness entangles its own self and therefore breathes not forth. Your reason, "If right will endures, by what justice can another's violence lessen the measure of my desert?" Further, that the souls appear to return to the stars, in accordance with Plato's teaching, gives you occasion for doubt. These are the questions that thrust equally upon your will. And therefore I will first treat that which has the most venom.

'Of the Seraphim he who is most in God, Moses, Samuel, and whichever John you will – I say, even Mary – have not their seats in any other heaven than these spirits which have now appeared to you, nor have they more or fewer years for their existence; but all make the first circle beautiful, and have sweet life in different measure, by feeling more and less the eternal breath. These showed themselves here, not because this sphere is allotted to them, but to afford sign of the celestial grade that is least exalted. It is needful to speak thus to your faculty, since only through sense perception does it apprehend that which it afterwards makes fit for the intellect. For this reason Scripture condescends to your capacity, and attributes hands and feet to God, having other meaning; and Holy Church represents to you with human aspect Gabriel and Michael and the other who made Tobit whole again. What Timaeus argues about the souls is not like this which is seen here, for seemingly he holds what he says for the truth. He says the soul returns to its own star, believing it to have been severed thence when nature gave it for a form. But perhaps his opinion is other than his words sound, and may be of a meaning not to be derided. If he means that the honor of their influence and the blame returns to these wheels, perhaps his bow hits some truth. This principle, ill-understood, once misled almost the entire world, so that it ran astray in naming Jove and Mercury and Mars.

'The other perplexity that troubles you has less of poison, for its malice could not lead you away from me elsewhere. For our justice to seem unjust in mortal eyes is argument of faith, not of heretical iniquity. But since your understanding can well penetrate to this truth, I will make you content as you desire.

'If it be violence when he who suffers contributes nothing to what forces him, these souls would not be excused on that account. For will, if it will not, is not quenched, but does as nature does in fire, though violence wrest it aside a thousand times. For should it bend itself much or little, it follows force: and thus did

these when they had power to return to the holy place. If their will had remained whole, such as held Lawrence on the grid and made Mucius severe to his own hand, it would have urged them back, so soon as they were loosed, by the road along which they had been dragged – but such sound will is all too rare. And by these words, if you have gathered them up as you should, is the argument quashed that would have troubled you yet many times.

'But now across your path another strait confronts your eyes, such that you would not get through it by yourself before you would be exhausted. I have put it in your mind for certain that a soul in bliss cannot lie, since it is always near the Primal Truth; and then you could hear from Piccarda that Constance kept her love for the veil, so that here she seems to contradict me. Many a time ere now, brother, has it happened that unwillingly, in order to escape from danger, that was done which ought not to have been done; even as Alcmeon who, urged thereto by his father, slew his own mother, and, so as not to fail in piety, became pitiless. At this point I would have you realize that force mixes with the will, and they so act that the offenses cannot be excused. Absolute will does not consent to the wrong, but the will consents thereto in so far as it fears, by drawing back, to fall into greater trouble. Therefore, when Piccarda says this, she means it of the absolute will, and I of the other; so that we both speak truth together.'

Such was the rippling of the holy stream which issued forth from the Fount from which springs every truth, and such it set at rest one and the other desire.

'O beloved of the First Lover, O divine one,' said I then, 'whose speech overflows me and warms me so that it quickens me more and more, not all the depth of my affection is sufficient to render to you grace for grace; but may He who sees and can answer thereto. Well do I see that never can our intellect be wholly satisfied unless that Truth shine on it, beyond which no truth has range. Therein it rests, as a wild beast in his lair, so soon as it has reached it; and reach it it can, else every desire would be in vain. Because of this questioning springs up like a shoot, at the foot of the truth; and this is

nature which urges us to the summit, from height to height. It is this, Lady, that invites and emboldens me to question you with reverence of another truth which is obscure to me. I wish to know if man can so satisfy you for broken vows, with other goods, as not to weigh too short upon your scales.'

Beatrice looked on me with eyes so full of the sparkling of love and so divine that my power, vanquished, took flight, and I almost lost myself with eyes downcast.

'IF I flame on you in the warmth of love beyond the measure that is seen on earth and so vanquish the power of your eyes, do not marvel, for it comes from perfect vision which, according as it apprehends, so does it move its foot to the apprehended good. Well do I note how in your intellect already is shining the eternal light which, seen, alone and always kindles love; and if aught else seduce your love, it is naught save some vestige of that light, ill-recognized, which therein shines through. You wish to know if for an unfulfilled vow so much can be paid with other service as may secure the soul from suit.'

So Beatrice began this canto, and as one who does not interrupt his speech, she thus continued her holy discourse, 'The greatest gift which God in His bounty bestowed in creating, and the most conformed to His own goodness and that which He most prizes, was the freedom of the will, with which the creatures that have intelligence, they all and they alone, were and are endowed. Now, if you argue from this, the high worth of the vow will appear to you, if it be such that God consents when you consent; for in establishing the compact between God and man, this treasure becomes the sacrifice, such as I pronounce it, and that by its own act. What then can be given in compensation? If you think to make good use of that which you have offered, you seek to do good with ill-gotten gains.

'You are now assured as to the greater point; but since Holy Church gives dispensation in this matter, which seems contrary to the truth I have declared to you, it behooves you to sit a while longer at table, for the tough food which you have taken requires still some aid for your digestion. Open your mind to that which I reveal to you, and fix it therewithin; for to have heard without retaining makes not knowledge.

'Two things constitute the essence of this sacrifice: the first is that in respect to which it is made, and the other is the covenant itself. This last is never canceled save by being kept, and concerning this was my preceding speech so precise. Therefore it was imperative upon the Hebrews to offer sacrifice in any case, though the thing offered might sometimes be changed, as you should know. The other, which is known to you as the matter, may indeed be such there is no fault if it be exchanged for other matter. But let no one shift the load upon his shoulder at his own judgment, without the turning of both the white and the yellow key; and let him hold all changing folly unless the thing laid down be not contained in that which is taken up, as four in six. Therefore, whatever thing weighs so much through its own worth as to tip every scale cannot be made good by any other outlay.

'Let mortals never take the vow in sport. Be faithful, and with that be not perverse, as was Jephthah in his first offering, who ought rather to have said 'I did amiss,' than, by keeping his vow, to do worse. And you can find the great leader of the Greeks in like manner foolish, wherefore Iphigenia wept that her face was fair, and made weep for her both the simple and the wise who heard the tale of such a rite. Be graver, you Christians, in moving. Be not like a feather to every wind, and think not that every water may cleanse you. You have the New Testament and the Old, and the Shepherd of the Church, to guide you: let this suffice for your salvation. If evil greed cry aught else to you, be you men, and not silly sheep, so that the Jew among you may not laugh at you. Be not like the lamb that leaves its mother's milk and, silly and wanton, fights with itself at its own pleasure.'

Thus Beatrice to me, even as I write; then she turned full of longing to that part where the universe is most alive. Her silence and her changed look imposed silence on my eager mind, which already had new questionings before it. And as an arrow that strikes the target

before the bowcord is quiet, so we sped into the second realm. Here I beheld my lady so glad, when she passed into that heaven's light, that the planet itself became the brighter for it; and if the star changed and smiled, what did I become, who by my very nature am subject to every kind of change?

As in a fish-pool that is still and clear the fish draw to that which comes in such manner from without that they deem it something they can feed on, so did I see full more than a thousand splendors draw towards us, and in each was heard, 'Lo one who shall increase our loves!' And, as each came up to us, the shade was seen full of joy, by the bright effulgence that issued from it.

Think, reader, if this beginning went no further, how you would feel an anguished craving to know more, and by yourself you will see what my desire was, to hear of their conditions from them, as soon as they became manifest to my eyes.

'O happy-born, to whom Grace concedes to see the thrones of the eternal triumph before you leave your time of warfare, we are enkindled by the light that ranges through all heaven; therefore, if you desire to draw light from us, sate yourself at your own pleasure.' Thus was it said to me by one of those devout spirits; and by Beatrice, 'Speak, speak securely, and trust even as to gods.'

'I see well how you do nest yourself in your own light, and that you dart it from your eyes, because it sparkles when you smile; but I know not who you are, nor why, O worthy spirit, you have your rank in the sphere that is veiled to mortals by another's rays.' This I said, turned toward the light which first had spoken to me; whereon it glowed far brighter than before. Even as the sun, which, when the heat has consumed the tempering of the dense vapors, conceals itself by excess of light, so, by reason of more joy, the holy figure hid itself from me within its own radiance and, thus close enclosed, it answered me in such fashion as the next canto sings.

'AFTER CONSTANTINE turned back the Eagle counter to the course of the heavens which it had followed behind the ancient who took Lavinia to wife, a hundred and a hundred years and more the bird of God abode on Europe's limit, near to the mountains from which it first had issued; and there it governed the world beneath the shadow of its sacred wings, from hand to hand, until by succeeding change it came into mine. I was Caesar, and am Justinian, who, by will of the Primal Love which I feel, removed from among the laws what was superfluous and vain. And before I had put my mind I held to be in Christ, and with that faith I was content; but the blessed Agapetus, who was the supreme pastor, directed me to the true faith by his words. I believed him, and what he held by faith I now see as clearly as you see that every contradiction is both false and true. So soon as with the Church I moved my feet, it pleased God, of His grace, to inspire me with this high task, and I gave myself entirely to it, committing arms to my Belisarius, with whom Heaven's right hand was so joined that it was a sign for me to rest from them.

'Here ends, then, my answer to the first question; but its condition constrains me to add a certain sequel to it, in order that you may see with how much reason they move against the sacred standard, both those that take it for their own and those that oppose it. See what great virtue made it worthy of reverence, beginning from the hour when Pallas died to give it sway. You know that it made its stay in Alba for three hundred years and more, till at the end, when the three fought against the three for it still. And you know what it did, through seven kings, from the wrong of the Sabine women down to the woe of Lucretia, conquering the neighboring people round about. You know what it did when borne by the illustrious Romans against Brennus, against Pyrrhus, and against the rest, princes and governments; whence Torquatus and Quinctius, named from his neglected locks, the Decii and the Fabii, acquired the fame which I gladly embalm. It cast down the pride of the Arabs that followed Hannibal across the Alpine rocks whence, Po, you do fall. Under it, Scipio and Pompey triumphed, while yet in their youth, and to that hill beneath which you were born it showed itself bitter. Afterward, near the time when all Heaven willed to bring the world to its own state of peace, Caesar, by the will of Rome, laid hold of it; and what it did from the Var even to the Rhine, the Isere beheld, and the Loire and the Seine beheld, and every valley whence Rhone is filled. What it did after it came forth from Ravenna and leaped the Rubicon was of such flight as no tongue nor pen might follow. Towards Spain it wheeled the host, then towards Durazzo, and did so smite Pharsalia that grief was felt on the burning Nile. It saw again Antandros and the Simois, whence it had set forth, and there where Hector lies; and then it shook itself again the worse for Ptolemy. From there it fell like lightning on Juba, then turned to your west, where it heard Pompey's trumpet. Of what it wrought with the succeeding marshal, Brutus and Cassius howl in Hell, and Modena and Perugia were doleful. Because of it sad Cleopatra is still weeping who, fleeing before it, took from the viper sudden and black death. With him it coursed far as the Red Sea Shore; with him it set the world in such peace that Janus's temple was locked.

'But what the standard that makes me speak had done before, and after was to do throughout the mortal realm subject unto it, becomes in appearance little and obscure if it be looked on in the hand of the third Caesar with clear eye and pure affection; because the living Justice which inspires me granted to it, in his hand of whom I speak, the glory of doing vengeance for Its own wrath. Now marvel here at what I unfold to you: afterwards it sped with Titus to do vengeance for the vengeance of the ancient sin. Then, when the Lombard tooth bit Holy Church, under its wings Charlemagne, conquering, succored her.

'Now you may judge of such as I accused but now, and of their offenses, which are the cause of all your ills. The one opposes to the public standard the yellow lilies, and the other claims it for a party, so that it is hard to see which offends the most. Let the Ghibellines, let

them practise their art under another ensign, for this one he ever follows ill who cleaves justice from it. And let not this new Charles strike it down with his Guelphs, but let him fear talons which have stripped the hide from a greater lion. Many a time ere now the sons have wept for the sin of the father; and let him not believe that God will change arms for his lilies.

'This little star is adorned with good spirits who have been active in order that honor and fame might come to them. And when desires, thus deviating, tend thitherward, the rays of true love must needs mount upwards less living. But in the equal measure of our rewards with our desert is part of our joy, because we see them neither less nor greater. Hereby the living Justice makes our affection so sweet within us that it can never be bent aside to any evil. Diverse voices make sweet music, so diverse ranks in our life render sweet harmony among these wheels.

'And within this present pearl shines the light of Romeo, whose noble and beautiful work was ill rewarded; but the Provençals who wrought against him have not the laugh, and indeed he takes an ill path who makes harm for himself of another's good work. Raymond Berenger had four daughters, each of them a queen, and Romeo, a man of lowly birth and a pilgrim, did this for him. And then crooked words moved him to demand a reckoning of this just man, who had rendered his seven and five for ten. Thereon he departed, poor and old, and if the world but knew the heart he had while begging his bread morsel by morsel, much as it praises him it would praise him more.'

CANTO VII

'*Hosanna, sanctus Deus sabaòth,*
superillustrans claritate tua
felices ignes horum malacòth!'
— so, revolving to his melody I saw that substance sing, on whom a double light is twinned; and he and the others moved in their dance, and like swiftest sparks veiled themselves from me by sudden distance. I was in doubt, and was saying to myself, 'Speak to her, speak to her,' I was saying, 'speak to her, to my

lady who slakes my thirst with her sweet distillings!' But that reverence which is wholly mistress of me, only by *Be* and by *ice*, bowed me like one who drowses. Short while did Beatrice suffer me thus, and she began, irradiating me with a smile such as would make a man happy in the fire, 'By my judgment, which cannot err, how just vengeance could be justly avenged, has set you pondering; but I will quickly free your mind, and do you listen, for my words will make you the gift of a great doctrine.

'By not enduring for his own good a curb upon the power that wills, that man who never was born, in damning himself damned all his progeny; wherefore the human race lay sick down there for many centuries in great error, until it pleased the word of God to descend where He, by the sole act of His eternal love, united with Himself in person the nature which had estranged itself from its Maker.

'Turn your sight now to that which now I say: this nature, which was thus united to its Maker, was, when it was created, pure and good; but by its own self it had been banished from Paradise, because it turned aside from the way of the truth and its proper life. The penalty therefore which the Cross inflicted, if it be measured by the nature assumed — none ever so justly stung; also none was ever of such great wrong, if we regard the Person who suffered it, with whom that nature was bound up. Therefore from one act issued things diverse, for one same death was pleasing to God and to the Jews; threat the earth trembled and Heaven was opened. No longer, now, should it seem hard to you when it is said that just vengeance was afterwards avenged by a just court.

'But now I see your mind from thought to thought entangled in a knot, from which, with great desire, it awaits release. You say, "I follow clearly what I hear, but why God willed this sole way for our redemption is hidden from me." This decree, brother, is buried from the eyes of everyone whose understanding is not matured within love's flame. But inasmuch as at this mark there is much aiming and little discernment, I shall tell why that way was the most fitting.

'The Divine Goodness, which spurns all envy from itself, burning within itself so sparkles that It displays the eternal beauties. That which immediately derives from it thereafter has no end, because when It seals, Its imprint may never be removed. That which rains down from it immediately is wholly free, because it is not subject to the power of the new things. It is the most conformed to it and therefore pleases It the most; for the Holy Ardor, which irradiates everything, is most living in what is most like Itself.

'With all these gifts the human creature is advantaged, and if one fails, it needs must fall from its nobility. Sin alone is that which disfranchises it and makes it unlike the Supreme Good, so that it is little illumined by Its light; and to its dignity it never returns unless, where fault has emptied, it fill up with just penalties against evil delight. Your nature, when it sinned totally in its seed, was removed from these dignities, even as from Paradise; nor could it recover them, if you consider carefully, by any way except the passing of one of these fords: either that God alone, solely by His clemency, had pardoned; or that man should of himself have given satisfaction for his folly. Fix your eyes now within the abyss of the Eternal Counsel, as closely fastened on my words as you are able. Man, within his own limits, could never make satisfaction, for not being able to descend in humility, by subsequent obedience, so far as in his disobedience he had intended to ascend; and this is the reason why man was shut off from power to make satisfaction by himself. Therefore it was needful for God, with His own ways, to restore man to his full life – I mean with one way, or else with both. But because the deed is so much the more prized by the doer, the more it displays of the goodness of the heart whence it issued, the divine Goodness which puts its imprint on the world, was pleased to proceed by all Its ways to raise you up again; nor between the last night and the first day has there been or will there be so exalted and so magnificent a procedure, either by one or by the other; for God was more bounteous in giving Himself to make man sufficient to uplift himself again, than if He solely of Himself had remitted; and all other modes were scanty in respect to justice, if the Son of God had not humbled himself to become incarnate.

'Now, to give full satisfaction to your every wish, I go back to explain to you a certain place, that you may see it as clearly as I do. You say, 'I see water, I see fire and air and earth, and all their mixtures come to corruption and endure but little, and yet these things were created things; so that, if what I have said to you be true, they ought to be secure against corruption.'

'The angels, brother, and the pure country in which you are, may be said to be created even as they are, may be said to be created even as they are, in their entire being; but the elements which you have named, and all things that are compounded of them, are informed by created power. Created was the matter that is in them, created was the informing virtue in these stars that wheel about them. The soul of every beast and of the plants is drawn from a potentiate compound by the shining and the motion of the holy lights; but your life the Supreme Benefi- cence breathes forth without intermediary, and so enamors it of Itself that it desires It ever after. And hence you further can infer your resurrec- tion, if you reflect how was the making of human flesh then when the first parents were both formed.'

CANTO VIII

THE WORLD was wont to believe, to its peril, that the fair Cyprian, wheeling in the third epicycle, rayed down mad love; wherefore the ancient people in their ancient error not only to her did honor with sacrifice and votive cry, but they honored Dione and Cupid, the one as her mother, the other as her son, and they told that he had sat in Dido's lap; and from her with whom I take my start they took the name of the star which the sun woos, now behind her, now before. I was not aware of rising into it, but of being within it my lady gave me full assurance when I saw her become more beautiful.

And as we see a spark within a flame, and as a voice within a voice is distinguished when one holds the note and another comes and goes, I saw within that light other lamps moving in a circle more and less swift according to the measure, I believe, of their internal sight. From a cold cloud winds, whether visible or not, never descended so swiftly that they would not seem impeded and slow to one who had seen those divine lights come to us, leaving the circling first begun among the high Seraphim; and within those that appeared most in front *Hosanna* sounded in such wise that never since have I been without the desire to hear it again.

Then one drew nearer to us, and alone began, 'We are all ready at your pleasure, that you may have joy of us. With one circle, with one circling and with one thirst we revolve with the celestial Princes to whom you in the world did once say, '*You who move the third heaven by intellection*'; and we are so full of love that, in order to please you, a little quiet will not be less sweet to us.'

After my eyes had been raised with rever- ence to my lady, and she had satisfied them with assurance of her consent, they turned back to the light which had promised so much; and 'Say who you are' was my utterance, stamped with great affection; and, how much I saw it increase in size and brightness, through the new joy which was added to its joys when I spoke! Thus changed, it said to me, 'The world held me below but little time; and had it been more, much ill shall be that would not have been. My joy, which rays around me, holds me concealed from you and hides me like a creature swathed in its own silk. Much did you love me, and had good cause; for had I remained below, I would have shown you of my love more than the leaves. That left bank which is bathed by the Rhone, after it has mingled with the Sorgue, awaited me in due time for its lord; so did that corner of Ausonia, down from where Tronto and Verde discharge into the sea, which is skirted by Bari and Gaeta and Catona. Already was shining on my brow the crown of that land which the Danube waters after it has left its German banks. And the fair Trinacria (which between Pachynus and Pelorus, on the gulf most vexed by Eurus, is darkened not by Typhoeus, but by nascent sulphur) would yet have looked to have its kings born through me from Charles and Rudolph, if ill lordship, which ever embitters the subject people, had not moved Palermo to shout, "Die! Die!" And if my brother foresaw this, he would already shun the rapacious poverty of Catalonia, lest it make trouble for him; for truly it is needful for him or for some other to look to it, lest upon his laden bark a heavier load be laid. His nature — mean descendant from a generous forebear — would need a knighthood that gave not its care to the filling of coffers.'

'Because I believe that the deep joy which your words infuse in me is, even as I see it, seen by you, my lord, there where every good has its end and its beginning, it is the more welcome to me; and this also I hold dear, that you discern it gazing upon God. You have made me glad; and so now do you make clear to me (since in speaking you have raised the question in my mind) how from sweet seed may come forth bitter.'

Thus I to him; and he to me, 'If I can make one truth plain to you, you will hold your face toward that which you ask, as you now hold your back. The Good which revolves and contents all the realm that you are climbing makes it providence become a power in these great bodies; and not only is the nature of things provided for in the Mind which by itself is perfect, but, along with that nature, their well-being; so that whatever this bow shoots falls disposed to a foreseen end, even as a shaft directed to its mark. Were this not so, the heavens which you are traversing would produce their effects in such wise that they would be not works of art but ruins — and that cannot be, unless the Intelligences that move these stars be defective, and defective also the Primal Intelligence in that it did not make them perfect. Do you wish this truth to be made still clearer to you?'

And I, 'No, truly; for I see it to be impossible that Nature should weary in that which is needful.'

Whereupon he again, 'Now say, would it be worse for man on earth if he were not a citizen?'

'Yes,' I replied, 'and here I ask for no proof.'

'And can that be, unless men below live in diverse ways for diverse duties? Not if your master writes well of this for you.' Thus he came deducing far as here, then he concluded, 'Therefore the roots of your works must need be diverse, so that one is born Solon and another

Xerxes, one Melchizedek and another he who flew through the air and lost his son. Circling nature, which is a seal on the mortal wax, performs its art well, but does not distinguish one house from another. Whence it happens that Esau differs in the seed from Jacob, and Quirinus comes from so base a father that he is ascribed to Mars. The begotten nature would always make its course like its begetters, did not Divine provision overrule.

Now that which was behind you is before you; but, that you may know that I delight in you, I will have a corollary cloak you round. Ever does Nature, if she find fortune discordant with herself, like any kind of seed out of its proper region, come to ill result. And if the world there below would give heed to the foundation which Nature lays, and followed it, it would have its people good. But you wrest to religion one born to gird on the sword, and you make a king of one that is fit for sermons; so that your track is off the road.'

CANTO IX

AFTER YOUR Charles, fair Clemence, had enlightened me, he told me of the frauds that his seed was destined to suffer, but he added, 'Keep silence, and let the years revolve'; so that I can say nothing except that well-deserved lamentation shall follow on the wrongs done you.

And now the life of that holy light had turned again to the Sun which fills it, as to that Good which is sufficient to all things. Ah, souls deceived and creatures impious, who from such Good turn away your hearts, directing your brows to vanity!

And lo! another of those splendors made toward me and by brightening outwardly was signifying its wish to please me. Beatrice's eyes, fixed on me as before, made me assured of dear assent to my desire.

'Pray, blessed spirit,' I said, 'afford speedy fulfillment to my wish, and give me proof that what I think I can reflect on you.' Whereon the light which was still new to me, from out of its depth where it first was singing, continued, as one rejoicing to do a kindness: 'In that region of the depraved land of Italy that lies between the

Rialto and the springs of the Brenta and the Piave there rises a hill of no great height, whence once descended a firebrand that made a great assault on the country round. I and he sprang from the same root. I was called Cunizza, and I am refulgent here because the light of this star overcame me. But I gladly pardon in myself the reason of my lot, and it does not grieve me — which might perhaps seem strange to your vulgar herd. Of this resplendent and precious jewel of our heaven which is nearest to me great fame has remained, and before it dies away this centennial year shall yet be fived. See if man should make himself excel, so that the first life may leave another after it! And this the present crowd which the Tagliamento and the Adige shut in considers not; nor yet, though it be scourged, does it repent. But soon it shall come to pass that, because her people are stubborn against duty, Padua at the marsh will stain the waters that bathe Vicenza. And where Sile joins Cagnano, one lords it and goes with his head high, for catching whom the web is already being made. Feltre shall yet bewail the crime of its impious shepherd, which will be so foul that for the like nobody ever entered Malta. Great indeed would be the vat that should receive the blood of the Ferrarese and weary him that should weigh it ounce by ounce, which this courteous priest will offer to show himself a member of his party — and such gifts will suit the country's way of life. Aloft are mirrors — you name them Thrones — whence God in judgment shines upon us, so that these words approve themselves to us.' Here she was silent, and had to me the semblance of being turned to other heeding, by the wheel in which she set herself as she was before.

The other joy, which was already known to me as precious, became to my sight like a fine ruby on which the sun is striking. Through rejoicing, effulgence is gained there on high, even as a smile here; but below, the shade darkens outwardly as the mind is sad.

'God sees all, and into Him your vision sinks, blessed spirit,' I said, 'so that no wish may steal itself from you. Why then does your voice, which ever gladdens Heaven — together with the singing of those devout fires that make themselves a cowl with the six wings – not satisfy my longings? Surely I should not wait for your request, were I in you, even as you are in me.'

'The greatest valley in which the water spreads from the sea that encircles the world,' he then began, 'extends its discordant shores so far counter to the sun that it makes meridian of the place where before it made horizon. I was a dweller on that valley's shore, between the Ebro and the Magra, which with short course divides the Genoese from the Tuscan; and with almost the same sunset and sunrise lie Bougie and the city whence I came, which with its own blood once made its harbor warm. Folco the people called me to whom my name was known, and this heaven is imprinted by me, as I was by it: for the daughter of Belus, wronging both Sichaeus and Creusa, burned not more than I, as long as it befitted my locks; nor yet the Rhodopean maid who was deluded by Demophoön, nor Alcides when he had enclosed Iole in his heart. Yet here we repent not, but we smile, not for the fault, which returns not to mind, but for the Power that ordained and foresaw. Here we contemplate the art which so much love adorns, and we discern the good by reason of which the world below again becomes the world above.

'But in order that you may bear away with you all your desires fulfilled which have been born in this sphere, I must proceed yet further. You wish to know who is within this light which so sparkles here beside me as a sunbeam on clear water. Now know that therewithin Rahab is at rest, and being joined with our order, it is sealed by her in the highest degree. By this heaven – in which the shadow that your earth casts comes to a point – she was taken up before any other soul of Christ's triumph. And it was well-befitting to leave her in some heaven as a trophy of the lofty victory which was achieved by the one and the other palm, because she favored Joshua's first glory in the Holy Land – which little touches the memory of the Pope.

'Your city – which was planted by him who first turned his back on his Maker, and whose envy has been so bewept – produces and scatters the accursed flower that has caused the sheep and the lambs to stray, because it has made a wolf of the shepherd. For this the Gospel and the great Doctors are deserted, and only the Decretals are studied, as may be seen by their margins. Thereon the Pope and Cardinals are intent. Their thoughts go not to Nazareth whither Gabriel spread his wings. But the Vatican and the other chosen parts of Rome which have been the burial place for the soldiery that followed Peter shall soon be free from this adultery.'

CANTO X

LOOKING UPON His Son with the love which the One and the Other eternally breathe forth, the primal and ineffable Power made everything that revolves through the mind or through space with such order that he who contemplates it cannot but taste of Him. Lift then your sight with me, reader, to the lofty wheels, straight to that part where the one motion strikes the other; and amorously there begin to gaze upon that a Master's art who within Himself so loves it that His eye never turns from it. See how from there the oblique circle which bears the planets branches off, to satisfy the world which calls on them: and were their pathway not aslant, much virtue in the heavens would be vain, and well-nigh every potency dead here below; and if it parted farther or less far from the straight course, much of the order of the world, both above and below, would be defective.

Now remain, reader, upon your bench, reflecting on this of which you have a foretaste, if you would be glad far sooner than weary. I have set before you; now feed yourself, because that matter of which I am made the scribe wrests to itself all my care.

The greatest minister of nature, which imprints the world with heavenly worth and with its light measures time for us, being in conjunction with the part I have noted, was wheeling through the spirals in which it presents itself earlier every day. And I was with him, but of my ascent I was no more aware than is a man, before his first thought, aware of its coming. It is Beatrice who thus conducts from good to better, so swiftly that her act does not extend through time.

How shining in itself must have been that which was within the sun where I entered it, showing not by color but by light! Though I should call on genius, art, and practice, I could not tell it so that it could ever be imagined; but one may believe it – and let him long to see it. And if our fantasies are low for such a loftiness, it is no marvel, for our eyes never knew a light brighter than the sun. Such was here the fourth family of the exalted Father who ever satisfies it, showing how He breathes forth, and how He begets. And Beatrice began, 'Give thanks, give thanks to the Sun of the Angels who of His grace has raised you to this visible one.'

Never was heart of mortal so disposed unto devotion and so ready, with all its gratitude, to give itself to God, as I became at those words. And all my love was so set on Him that it eclipsed Beatrice in oblivion; nor did this displease her, but she so smiled thereat that the splendor of her smiling eyes divided upon many things my mind intent on one.

I saw many flashing lights of surpassing brightness make of us a center and of themselves a crown, more sweet in voice than shining in aspect. Thus girt we sometimes see Latona's daughter when the air is so impregnate that it holds the thread which makes her zone. In the court of Heaven, whence I have returned, are many gems so precious and beautiful that they may not be taken out of the kingdom, and of these was the song of those lights. Let him who does not wing himself so that he may fly up thither await tidings thence from the dumb.

When, so singing, those blazing suns had circled three times round about us, like stars neighboring the fixed poles, they seemed as ladies not released from the dance, but who stop silent, listening till they have caught the new notes. And within one I heard begin, 'Since the ray of grace, by which true love is kindled and which then grows by loving, shines so multiplied in you that it brings you up that stair which none descends but to mount again, he who should deny to you the wine of his flask for your thirst would no more be at liberty than water that flows not down to the sea. You wish to know what plants these are that enflower this garland, which amorously circles round the fair lady who strengthens you for heaven. I was of the lambs of the holy flock which Dominic leads on the path where there is good fattening if they do not stray. He that is next beside me on the right was my brother and my master, and he is Albert of Cologne, and I Thomas of Aquino. If thus of all the rest you would be informed, come, following my speech with your sight, going round the blessed wreath. The next flaming comes from the smile of Gratian who served the one and the other court so well that it pleases in Paradise. The other who next adorns our choir was that Peter who, like the poor widow, offered his treasure to Holy Church. The fifth light, which is the most beautiful among us, breathes with such love that all the world there below thirsts to know tidings of it. Within it is the lofty mind to which was given wisdom so deep that, if the truth be true, there never rose a second of such full vision. At its side behold the light of that candle which, below in the flesh, saw deepest into the angelic nature and its ministry. In the next little light smiles that defender of the Christian times, of whose discourse Augustine made use. If now you are bringing your mind's eye from light to light after my praises, you are already thirsting for the eighth. Therewithin, through seeing every good, the sainted soul rejoices who makes the fallacious world manifest to any who listen well to him. The body from which it was driven lies down below in Cieldauro, and he came from martyrdom and exile to this peace. See, flaming beyond, the glowing breath of Isidore, of Bede, and of Richard who in contemplation was more than man. This one from whom your look returns to me is the light of a spirit to whom, in his grave thoughts, it seemed that death came slow. It is the eternal light of Siger who, lecturing in Straw Street, demonstrated invidious truths.'

Then, like a clock which calls us at the hour when the Bride of God rises to sing her matins to her Bridegroom, that he may love her, in which the one part draws or drives the other, sounding *ting! ting!* with notes so sweet that well-disposed spirit swells with love, so did I see the glorious wheel move and render voice to voice with harmony and sweetness that cannot be known except there where joy is everlasting.

CANTO XI

O INSENSATE care of mortals! how false are the reasonings that make you beat your wings in downward flight. One was following after the laws, another after the *Aphorisms*, one was pursuing priesthood, and one dominion by force or craft, and another plunder, and another civil business, one was moiling, caught in the pleasures of the flesh, and another was giving himself to idleness, the while, free from all these things, I was high in heaven with Beatrice, thus gloriously received.

After each had come to the point of the circle where it was before, it stayed itself, as the taper in its stand. And within that light which first had spoken to me I heard begin, while it smiled and grew brighter, 'Even as I glow with its beams, so, gazing into the Eternal Light, I perceive your thoughts and the cause of them. You are perplexed and would fain have my words made clearer, in plain and explicit language leveled to your understanding, where I said just now "where there is good fattening," and again where I said, "there never rose a second"; and here is need that one distinguish well.

'The Providence that governs the world with that counsel in which every created vision is vanquished before it reaches the bottom, in order that the Bride of Him who, with loud cries, espoused her with the blessed blood, might go to her Delight, secure within herself and also more faithful to Him, ordained on her behalf two princes, who on this side and that might be her guides. The one was all seraphic in ardor, the other, for wisdom, was on earth a splendor of cherubic light. I will speak of one, because in praising one, whichever be taken, both are spoken of, for their labors were to one same end.

'Between the Topino and the stream that drops from the hill chosen by the blessed Ubaldo, a fertile slope hangs from a lofty mountain wherefrom Perugia feels cold and heat through Porta Sole, while behind it Nocera and Gualdo grieve under a heavy yoke.

From this slope, where most it breaks its steepness a sun rose on the world, even as this is wont to rise from Ganges. Therefore let him who talks of this place not say *Ascesi*, which would be to speak short, but *Orient*, if he would name it rightly. He was not yet very far from his rising when he began to make the earth feel, from his great virtue, a certain strengthening; for, while still a youth, he rushed into strife against his father for such a lady, to whom, as to death, none willingly unlocks the door; and before his spiritual court *et coram patre* he was joined to her, and thereafter, from day to day, he loved her ever more ardently. She, bereft of her first husband, for eleven hundred years and more, despised and obscure, remained unwooed till he came; nor had it availed to hear that he who caused fear to all the world found her undisturbed with Amyclas at the sound of his voice; nor had it availed to have been constant and undaunted so that, where Mary remained below, she wept with Christ upon the Cross.

'But, lest I should proceed too darkly, take now Francis and Poverty for these lovers in all that I have said. Their harmony and joyous semblance made love and wonder and tender looks the cause of holy thoughts; so that the venerable Bernard first bared his feet, following such great peace, and running, it seemed to him that he was slow. Oh wealth unknown, oh fertile good! Egidius bares his feet, Silvester bares his feet, following the spouse, so does the bride delight them. Then that father and master goes his way, with his lady and with that family which was already girt with the lowly cord. Nor did abjectness of heart weigh down his brow that he was Pietro Bernardone's son, nor for appearing marvelously despised; but royally he opened his stern resolve to Innocent, and had from him the first seal upon his Order.

'After the poor folk had increased behind him, whose wondrous life were better sung in Heaven's glory, then was the holy will of this chief shepherd circled with a second crown by the Eternal Spirit through Honorius. And when, in thirst for martyrdom, he, in the proud presence of the Sultan, had preached Christ and them that followed him, and, finding the people too unripe for conversion and in order not to stay in vain, had returned to the harvest of the Italian fields, then on the harsh rock between Tiber and Arno he received from Christ the last seal, which his limbs bore for two years. When it pleased Him, who had allotted him to such great good, to draw him up to the reward that he had gained in making himself lowly, to his brethren as to rightful heirs he commended his most dear lady and bade them love her faithfully; and from her bosom the glorious soul chose to set forth, returning to its own realm, and for its body would have no other bier.

'Think now what he was that was a worthy colleague to keep Peter's bark on the right course in the high sea; and such was our Patriarch; wherefore you can see that whoever follows him as he commands freights good merchandise. But his flock has grown so greedy of new fare that it cannot but be scattered through wild pastures; and the farther his sheep, remote and vagabond, go from him, the more empty of milk do they return to the fold. Some of them indeed there are who fear the harm, and keep close to the shepherd, but they are so few that little cloth suffices for their cowls.

'Now if my words have not been faint, if your listening has been intent, if you recall to mind what I have said, your wish will be content in part, for you will see the plant which is whittled away, and you will see what is intended by the correction "where there is good fattening if they do not stray."'

CANTO XII

As soon as the blessed flame took to speaking its last word the holy millstone began to turn, and it had not yet made a full circle when a second enclosed it round and matched motion with motion and song with song: song which, in those sweet pipes, as much surpasses our Muses, our Sirens, as a first splendor that which it throws back. As two bows, parallel and like in color, bend across a thin cloud when Juno gives the order to her handmaid — the one without born of the one within, like the voice of that wandering nymph whom love consumed as the sun does vapors — and make the people here presage, by reason of

the covenant that God made with Noah, that the world shall never again be flooded; so the two garlands of those sempiternal roses circled round us, and so did the outer correspond to the inner.

When the dance and all the great festival of both song and flames, light with light, gladsome and benign, stopped together at one instant and with one consent (even as the eyes which, at the pleasure that moves them, must needs be closed and lifted in accord), from the heart of one of the new lights there came a voice which made me seem as the needle to the star in turning me to where it was; and it began, 'The love that makes me beautiful draws me to speak of the other leader on whose account such fair utterance is made here concerning mine. It is fit that where one is, the other be brought in, so that, as they warred for one same end, so together may their glory shine.

'Christ's army, which cost so dear to rearm, was moving behind the standard, slow, mistrustful and scanty, when the Emperor who reigns eternally took thought for His soldiery that was in peril, of His grace only, not that it was worthy, and, as has been said, succored His bride with two champions by whose deeds, by whose words, the scattered people were rallied.

'In that region where sweet Zephyr rises to open the new leaves wherewith Europe sees herself reclad, not far from the smiting of the waves, behind which the sun, after his long course, sometimes hides himself from every man, sits fortunate Calaroga under the protection of the mighty shield whereon the lion is subject and sovereign. Therein was born the ardent lover of the Christian faith, the holy athlete, benignant to his own and harsh to his foes. And his mind, as soon as it was created, was so full of living virtue that in his mother's womb he made her a prophetess. When the espousals were completed at the sacred font between him and the faith, where they dowered each other with mutual salvation, the lady who gave the assent for him saw in a dream the marvelous fruit destined to issue from him and from his heirs, and, that he might in very construing be what he was, a spirit from up here went forth to name him by the possessive of

Him whose he wholly was. Dominic he was named, and I speak of him as of the husbandman whom Christ chose to help Him in His garden. Well did he show himself a messenger and familiar of Christ; for the first love manifested in him was for the first counsel that Christ gave. Oftentimes his nurse found him silent and awake upon the ground, as though he would say, "I am come for this." Oh father of him, Felice indeed! Oh mother of him, Giovanna indeed, if this, being interpreted, means as is said!

'Not for the world for whose sake men now toil after him of Ostia and after Thaddeus, but for love of the true manna, in short time he became a mighty teacher, such that he set himself to go round the vineyard, which soon turns gray if the vine-dresser is negligent. And of the seat which once was more benign to the righteous poor — not in itself, but in him who sits on it and degenerates — he asked, not to dispense two or three for six, not for the fortune of the first vacancy, not for *decimas quae sunt pauperum Dei*, but for leave to fight against the erring world for that seed of which four and twenty plants surround you. Then both with doctrine and with will, together with the apostolic office, he went forth like a torrent which a lofty vein presses out, and on the heretical stocks his force struck with most vigor where the resistances were most obstinate. From him there sprang then various streamlets whereby the catholic garden is watered, so that its bushes are more living.

'If such was the one wheel of the chariot in which Holy Church defended herself and won in the field her civil strife, surely the excellence of the other must be very plain to you, concerning whom, before I came, Thomas was so courteous. But the track made by the topmost part of its rim is derelict; so that there is mould where the crust was. His household, which set out aright with their feet upon his footprints, is so turned about that the forward foot moves to that behind; and soon shall be seen some harvest of the bad tillage, when the tare will complain that the bin is taken from it. Nevertheless, I say, he who should search our volume leaf by leaf might still find a page where he would read, "I am as I always was"; but it will not be from Casale or from Acquasparta, whence come such to the writing that one shuns it and the other contracts it.

'I am the living soul of Bonaventura of Bagnorea, who in the great offices always put the left-hand care behind. Illuminato and Augustine are here, who were of the first unshod poor brethren that with the cord made themselves God's friends. Hugh of St. Victor is here with them, and Peter Comestor, and Peter of Spain, who down below shines in twelve books; Nathan the prophet, and the Metropolitan Chrysostom, and Anselm, and that Donatus who deigned to set his hand to the first art; Rabanus is here, and beside me shines the Calabrian abbot Joachim, who was endowed with prophetic spirit.

'The glowing courtesy and the well-judged discourse of Brother Thomas has moved me to celebrate so great a paladin, and with me has moved this company.'

CANTO XIII

LET HIM imagine, who would rightly grasp what I now beheld (and, while I speak, let him hold the image firm as a rock), fifteen stars which in different regions vivify the heaven with such great brightness that it overcomes every thickness of the air; let him imagine that Wain for which the bosom of our heaven suffices night and day so that with the turning of the pole it does not disappear; let him imagine the mouth of that Horn which begins at the end of the axle on which the first wheel revolves — all to have made of themselves two signs in the heavens like that which the daughter of Minos made when she felt the chill of death; and one to have its rays within the other, and both to revolve in such manner that one should go first and the other after; and he will have as it were a shadow of the true constellation, and of the double dance, which was circling round the point where I was; for it is as far beyond our experience as the motion of the heaven that outspeeds all the rest is beyond the motion of the Chiana. There they sang not Bacchus, and not Paean, but Three Persons in the divine nature, and it and the human nature in one Person. The singing and the circling

completed each its measure, and those holy lights gave heed to us, rejoicing as they passed from care to care.

Then the light within which the wondrous life of the poor man of God had been narrated to me broke the silence among the concordant souls, and said, 'Since one straw is threshed, since its grain is now garnered, sweet charity bids me beat out the other. You believe that into the breast from which the rib was drawn to form her beautiful cheek whose palate costs dear to all the world, and into that which, pierced by the lance, made such satisfaction, both after and before, that it turns the scale against all fault, whatever of light it is allowed human nature to have was all infused by that Power which made the one and the other; and therefore you wonder at what I said above, when I declared that the excellence which is enclosed in the fifth light never had a second. Now open your eyes to that which I answer you, and you will see your belief and what I say become in the truth as the center in a circle.

'That which dies not and that which can die are naught but the splendor of that Idea which in His love our Sire begets; for that living light which so streams from its Lucent Source that It is not disunited from It, nor from the Love which is intrined with them, does of Its own goodness collect Its rays, as though reflected, in nine subsistences, Itself eternally remaining One. Thence It descends to the ultimate potentialities, downward from act to act becoming such that finally it makes but brief contingencies; and these contingencies I understand to be the generated things which the moving heavens produce with seed and without it. The wax of these and that which molds it are not always in the same condition, and therefore under the ideal stamp it then shines now more, now less, hence it comes that one same plant, in respect to species, fruits better or worse, and that you are born with diverse dispositions. If the wax were exactly worked, and the heavens were at the height of their power, the light of the whole seal would be apparent. But nature always gives it defectively, working like the artist who in the practice of his art has a hand that trembles. Yet, if the fervent Love disposes and imprints the clear Vision of

the primal Power, complete perfection is there acquired. Thus was the dust once made fit for the full perfection of a living creature, thus was the Virgin made to be with child; so that I approve your opinion that human nature never was, nor shall be, what it was in those two persons.

'Now, if I went no further, "How, then, was that other without an equal?" would your words begin. But in order that that which is not apparent may clearly appear, consider who he was and the cause which moved him to make request when it was said to him, "Ask." I have not so spoken that you cannot plainly see that he was a king, who asked for wisdom, in order that he might be a worthy king; not to know the number of the mover spirits here above, nor if *necesse* with a contingent ever made *necesse*; nor *si est dare primum motum esse*; nor if in a semicircle a triangle can be so constructed that it shall have no right angle. Wherefore, if you note this along with what I said, kingly prudence is that peerless vision on which the arrow of my intention strikes. And if to 'rose' you turn your discerning eyes, you will see it has respect only to kings — who are many and the good are rare. Take my words with this distinction, and they can stand thus with what you believe of the first father and of our Beloved.

'And let this ever be as lead to your feet, to make you slow, like a weary man, in moving either to the *yes* or the *no* which you see not; for he is right low down among the fools, alike in the one and in the other case, who affirms or denies without distinguishing; because it happens that oftentimes hasty opinion inclines to the wrong side, and then fondness for it binds the intellect. Far worse than in vain does he leave the shore (since he returns not as he puts forth) who fishes for the truth and has not the art. And of this Parmenides, Melissus, Bryson, are open proofs to the world, as are the many others who went on but knew not whither. Thus did Sabellius, and Arius, and those fools who were to the Scriptures like swords, in rendering straight countenances distorted.

Moreover, let folk not be too secure in judgment, like one who should count the ears in the field before they are ripe; for I have seen first, all winter through, the thorn display itself hard and stiff, and then upon its summit bear the rose. And I have seen ere now a ship fare straight and swift over the sea through all her course, and perish at the last as she entered the harbor. Let not dame Bertha and squire Martin, if they see one steal and one make offering, believe to see them within the Divine Counsel: for the one may rise and the other may fall.'

Canto XIV

FROM THE center to the rim, and so from the rim to the centre, the water in a round vessel moves, according as it is struck from without or within. This which I say fell suddenly into my mind as the glorious life of Thomas became silent, because of the likeness which was born of his speech and that of Beatrice, who was pleased to begin thus after him, 'This man has need, and does not tell you of it, either by word or as yet in thought, to go to the root of another truth. Tell him if the light wherewith your substance blooms will remain with you eternally even as it is now; and, if it does remain, tell how, after you are made visible again, it can be that it will not hurt your sight.'

As when urged and drawn on by increasing delight, those who are dancing in a ring from time to time raise their voices and gladden their motions, so at that prompt and devout petition the holy circles showed new joy in their revolving and in their marvelous melody. Whoso laments because we die here to live there on high has not seen there the refreshment of the eternal rain.

That One and Two and Three which ever lives, and ever reigns in Three and Two and One, uncircumscribed, and circumscribing all things, was thrice sung by each of those spirits with such a melody as would be adequate reward for every merit. And I heard in the divinest light of the lesser circle a modest voice, perhaps such as was that of the Angel to Mary, make answer, 'As long as the feast of Paradise shall be, so long shall our love radiate around us such a garment. Its brightness follows our ardor, the ardor our vision, and that is in the measure which each has of grace beyond his merit. When the flesh, glorious and sanctified,

shall be clothed on us again, our persons will be more acceptable for being all complete; wherefore whatever of gratuitous light the Supreme Good gives us will be increased, light which fits us to see Him; so that our vision needs must increase, our ardor increase which by that is kindled, our radiance increase which comes from this. But even as a coal which gives forth flame, and with its white glow outshines it, so that its visibility is maintained, so shall this effulgence which already surrounds us be surpassed in brightness by the flesh which the earth still covers; nor will such light have power to fatigue us, for the organs of the body will be strong for everything that can delight us.'

So sudden and eager both the one and the other chorus seemed to me in saying 'Amen,' that truly they showed desire for their dead bodies – perhaps not only for themselves, but also for their mothers, for their fathers, and for the others who were dear before they became eternal flames.

And lo! round about and of equal brightness rose a lustre beyond that which was there, like a brightening horizon. And as, at rise of early evening, new lights begin to show in heaven, so that the sight does, and yet does not, seem real, it seemed to me that there I began to perceive new subsistences making a ring beyond the other two circumferences. Oh true sparkling of the Holy Spirit! how suddenly glowing it became to my eyes, which, vanquished, endured it not. But Beatrice showed. herself to me so beautiful and smiling that it must be left among those sights which followed not my memory. Therefrom my eyes regained power to raise themselves again, and I saw myself, alone with my lady, translated to a more exalted blessedness. That I was more uplifted I perceived clearly by the fiery smile of the star which seemed to me ruddier than its wont. With all my heart, and with that speech which is one in all men, I made a holocaust to God such as befitted the new grace; and the burning of the sacrifice was not yet completed in my breast when I knew the offering to be accepted and propitious, for with such a glow and such a ruddiness splendors appeared to me within two rays that I said, 'O Helios, who dost so adorn them!'

As, pricked out with greater and lesser lights, between the poles of the Universe, the Milky Way so gleams as to cause even the wise to question, so did those beams, thus constellated, make in the depth of Mars the venerable sign which joinings of quadrants make in a circle. Here my memory outstrips my wit, for that Cross so flashed forth Christ that I can find for it no fit comparison; but he that takes up his cross and follows Christ shall yet forgive me for what I leave untold when he sees Christ flash in that dawn.

From horn to horn and between the top and the base, lights were moving that sparkled brightly as they met and passed; so we see here, straight and athwart, swift and slow, changing appearance, the motes of bodies, long and short, moving through the ray that sometimes streaks the shade which men with skill and art contrive for their defense. And as viol and harp, strung with many cords in harmony, chime sweetly for one who does not catch the tune, so from the lights that appeared to me there a melody gathered through the cross which held me rapt, though I followed not the hymn. Well I discerned it to be of lofty praise, for there came to me: 'Rise' and 'Conquer,' as to one who understands not, but hears; by which I was so moved to love that till then nothing had bound me with such sweet bonds. Perhaps my word appears too daring, as though slighting the pleasure of the beautiful eyes, gazing into which my longing has repose. But he who considers that the living seals of every beauty have more effect the higher they are, and that I there had not yet turned to them, may excuse me for that whereof I accuse myself in order to excuse myself, and may see that I speak truth; for the holy pleasure is not excluded here, because it becomes the purer as one mounts.

Canto XV

GRACIOUS WILL, wherein right-breathing love always resolves itself, as cupidity does into grudging will, imposed silence on that sweet lyre and quieted the holy strings which the right hand of Heaven slackens and draws tight. How shall those beings be deaf to righteous prayers, who, in order to prompt me to beg of them, became silent with one consent? Right it is that he should grieve without end who, for the love of what does not endure forever, robs himself of that love.

As, through the still and cloudless evening sky a sudden fire shoots from time to time, moving the eyes that were at rest, and seeming a star that changes place, save that from where it kindles no star is lost, and it lasts but short while; so, from the horn that extends on the right, there darted a star of the resplendent constellation that is there, down to the foot of that cross; nor did the gem depart from its ribbon, but coursed along the radial strip, and seemed like fire behind alabaster. With like affection did the shade of Anchises stretch forward (if our greatest Muse merits belief), when in Elysium he perceived his son.

'O sanguis meus, O superinfusa gratia Dei, sicut tibi cui bis unquam celi ianua reclusa?' Thus that light; wherefore I gave my heed to it, then I turned back my sight to my lady, and on this side and that I was amazed, for in her eyes was blazing such a smile that I thought with mine I had touched the limit both of my beatitude and of my paradise.

Then, a joy to hearing and to sight, the spirit added to his first words things I did not comprehend, so deep was his speech; nor did he conceal himself from me by choice, but of necessity, for his conception was set above the mark of mortals. And when the bow of his ardent affection was so relaxed that his speech descended toward the mark of our intellect, the first thing I understood was, 'Blessed be Thou, Three and One, who show such favor to my seed.' And he continued, 'Happy and long-felt hunger, derived from reading in the great volume where white or dark is never changed, you have relieved, my son, within this light in which I speak to you, thanks to her who clothed you with plumes for the lofty flight. You believe that your thought flows to me from Him who is First, even as from the unit, if that be known, ray out the five and the six; and therefore who I am, and why I seem to you more joyous than another in this festive throng, you do not ask me. You believe the truth, for the lesser and the great of this life gaze into that mirror in which, before you think, you display

your thought. But in order that holy love, in which I watch with perpetual vision, and which makes me thirst with sweet longing, may be the better fulfilled, let your voice, confident and bold and glad, sound forth the will, sound forth the desire, whereto my answer is already decreed.'

I turned to Beatrice, and she heard before I spoke, and smiled to me a sign that made the wings of my desire increase. And I began thus, 'Love and intelligence, as soon as the first Equality became visible to you, became of one weight for each of you, because the Sun which illumined you and warmed you is of such equality in its heat and light that all comparisons fall short. But will and faculty in mortals, for the reason that is plain to you, are not equally feathered in their wings, so that I, who am mortal, feel myself in this inequality, and therefore can only give thanks with the heart for your paternal welcome. But I beseech you, living topaz who are a gem in this precious jewel, that you satisfy me with your name.'

'O my branch, in whom I took delight only expecting you, I was your root.' Thus he began his answer to me, then said, 'He from whom your family has its name and who a hundred years and more has circled the mountain on the first ledge, was my son and was your grandfather's father. Truly it is fitting that you should shorten his long toil with your good offices.

'Florence, within her ancient circle from which she still takes tierce and nones, abode in peace, sober and chaste. There was no necklace, no coronal, no embroidered gowns, no girdle that was more to be looked at than the person. Not yet did the daughter at her birth cause fear to the father, for the time and the dowry did not outrun due measure on this side and that. Houses empty of family there were none, nor had Sardanapalus arrived yet to show what could be done in the chamber. Not yet was Montemalo surpassed by your Uccellatoio, which, as it has been passed in the uprising, so shall it be in the fall. Bellincion Berti have I seen go girt with leather and bone, and his wife come from her mirror with unpainted face. I have seen de' Nerli and del Vecchio content in unlined skin, and their wives at the spindle and the distaff. O happy they! each one of them sure

of her burial place, and none as yet deserted in her bed because of France. The one kept watch in minding the cradle, and, soothing, spoke that speech which first delights fathers and mothers. Another, as she drew the threads from the distaff, would tell her household about the Trojans, and Fiesole, and Rome. Then a Cianghella or a Lapo Salterello would have been as great a marvel as Cincinnatus and Cornelia would be now.

'To so reposeful, to so fair a life of citizens, to such a trusty community, to so sweet an abode, Mary, called on with loud cries, gave me, and in your ancient Baptistery I became at once a Christian and Cacciaguida. Moronto was my brother, and Eliseo. My wife came to me from the valley of the Po, and thence was derived your surname. Afterward I followed the Emperor Conrad, who girt me with his knighthood, so much did I win his favor by good work. I went, in his train, against the iniquity of that law whose people, through fault of the Pastors, usurp your right. There by that foul folk was I released from the deceitful world, the love of which debases many souls, and I came from martyrdom to this peace.'

CANTO XVI

O OUR petty nobility of blood! if you make folk glory in you here below where our affections languish, it will nevermore be a marvel to me, since there where appetite is not warped, I mean in Heaven, I myself gloried in you. Truly you are a mantle that soon shrinks, so that if naught be added from day to day, time goes round about you with its shears.

With that *You* which was first used in Rome and in which her family least perseveres, my words began again; at which Beatrice, who was a little withdrawn, smiled and seemed to me like her who coughed at the first fault that is written of Guinevere. I began, 'You are my father, you give me full boldness to speak, you so uplift me that I am more than I. By so many streams my mind is filled with gladness that it rejoices in itself that it can bear this and not burst. Tell me then, dear stock from which I spring, what was your ancestry and what were the years that were reckoned in your boyhood.

Tell me of the sheepfold of St. John, how large it was then, and who were the folk within it worthy of the highest seats.'

As a coal quickens into flame at the breathing of the winds, so did I see that light glow at my blandishments; and as it became more beautiful to my eyes, so with a voice more sweet and gentle, but not in this our modern speech, he said to me, 'From that day on which *Ave* was uttered, to the birth in which my mother, who now is sainted, was lightened of me with whom she had been burdened, this fire had come to its Lion five hundred, fifty, and thirty times to rekindle itself beneath his paw. My ancestors and I were born at the place where the furthest ward is first reached by the runner in your annual game. Let it suffice to hear thus much of forebears; as to who they were and whence they came hither, silence is more becoming than speech.

'All those able to bear arms who at that time were there, between Mars and the Baptist, were the fifth of the number now living; but the citizenship, which is now mixed with Campi, with Certaldo, and with Figline, saw itself pure down to the humblest artisan. Oh, how much better it would be that those folk of whom I speak were neighbors, and to have your boundary at Galluzzo and at Trespiano, than to have them within and to endure the stench of the churl of Aguglione, and of him of Signa, who already has his sharp eye for jobbery.

'If the folk who are the most degenerate in the world had not been a stepmother to Caesar, but, like a mother, benignant to her son, there is one who has become a Florentine and is a money-changer and trader, who would have lived on at Simifonti where his own grand-father went a-begging. Montemurlo would still belong to its Counts, the Cerchi would be in the parish of Acone, and perhaps the Buondel-monti in Valdigreve. The intermingling of people was ever the beginning of harm to the city, as to you the food which is loaded on is to the body. And a blind bull falls more headlong than the blind lamb, and oftentimes one sword cuts better and more than five.

'If you regard Luni and Urbisaglia, how they have perished, and how are following after

them Chiusi and Senigallia, it will not appear to you a strange thing or a hard, to hear how families are undone, since cities have their term. Your affairs all have their death, even as have you; but it is concealed in some things that last long, whereas lives are short. And as the revolution of the heaven of the moon covers and uncovers the shores without pause, so Fortune does with Florence; wherefore it should appear no wondrous thing which I shall tell of the great Florentines whose fame is hidden by time. I saw the Ughi and I saw the Catellini, Filippi, Greci, Ormanni, and Alberichi, illustrious citizens, already in decline; and I saw, great as they were ancient, dell'Arca with della San-nella, and Soldanieri and Ardinghi and Bostichi. Over the gate which at present is laden with new felony of such great weight that there will soon be jettison from the bark, were the Ravignani of whose line the Count Guido is descended and whosoever has since taken the name of the high Bellincione. Della Pressa knew already how to rule, and Galligaio had already in his house the hilt and the pommel gilded. Great already were the Vair column, the Sacchetti, Giuochi, Fifanti, Barucci, and Galli, and those that blush for the bushel. The stock from which the Calfucci sprang was already great, and already the Sizii and Arrigucci had been raised to the highest seats. Oh, how great have I seen those now undone by their pride! and the balls of gold adorned Florence in all her great doings. So did the fathers of those who, whenever your church is vacant, fatten themselves by staying in consis-tory. The insolent breed that plays the dragon behind him that flees, and to whoever shows his teeth – or else his purse – becomes mild as a lamb, was already on the rise, but of humble stock, so that it did not please Ubertin Donato that his father-in-law afterward should make him their kinsman. Already had Caponsacco descended into the market-place down from Fiesole, and already was Giuda a good citizen, and Infangato. One thing I will tell, incredible and true: the little circuit was entered by a gate named after the Della Pera. Everyone who bears the fair ensign of the great Baron whose name and whose worth the feast of Thomas keeps fresh, from him had knighthood and

privilege, although he who fringes it round is siding now with the people. Already there were Gualterotti and Importuni; and the Borgo would still be quiet if they had gone fasting of new neighbors. The house of which was born your weeping, by reason of its just resentment which has slain you and put an end to your glad living, was honored, both itself and its consorts. O Buondelmonte, how ill for you that you did fly from its nuptials at the promptings of another. Many would be happy who now are sad if God had committed you to the Ema the first time you came to the city! but it was fitting that Florence, in her last peace, should offer a victim to that mutilated stone which guards the bridge.

'With these families, and with others with them, I saw Florence in such repose that she had no cause for wailing. With these families I saw her people so glorious and so just, that the lily was never set reversed upon the staff, nor made vermilion by division.'

CANTO XVII

AS HE who still makes fathers chary toward their sons came to Clymene to be reassured about that which he had heard against himself, such was I, and such was I perceived to be both by Beatrice and by the holy lamp which already, for my sake, had changed its place. Wherefore my lady said to me, 'Put forth the flame of your desire, so that it may issue imprinted well by the internal stamp; not in order that our knowledge may increase through your speech, but that you may learn to tell your thirst, so that one may pour out drink for you.'

'O dear root of me, who are so uplifted that, even as earthly minds see that two obtuse angles can not be contained in a triangle, so you, gazing upon the Point to which all times are present, do see contingent things before they exist in themselves; while I was in Virgil's company, up the mountain that heals the souls, and while descending through the dead world, heavy words were said to me about my future life, though I feel myself truly foursquare against the blows of chance; so that my will would be well content to hear what fortune is drawing near me, because an arrow foreseen comes slower.' Thus said I to that same light which had spoken to me before, and, as Beatrice willed, my wish was confessed.

In no dark sayings, such as those in which the foolish folk of old once ensnared themselves, before the Lamb of God who takes away sins was slain, but in clear words and with precise discourse that paternal love replied, hidden and revealed by his own smile, 'Contingency, which does not extend beyond the volume of your material world, is all depicted in the Eternal Vision. Yet thence it takes not necessity, any more than from the eyes in which it is mirrored does a ship which is going down the stream. Therefrom, even as sweet harmony comes from an organ to the ear, comes to my sight the time that is in store for you. As Hippolytus departed from Athens, by reason of his pitiless and perfidious stepmother, so from Florence must you depart. So is it willed, so already plotted, and so shall be accomplished soon by him who ponders upon it in the place where every day Christ is bought and sold. The blame, as always, will follow the injured party, in outcry; but vengeance shall bear witness to the truth which dispenses it. You shall leave everything beloved most dearly; and this is the arrow which the bow of exile shoots first. You shall come to know how salt is the taste of another's bread, and how hard the path to descend and mount by another man's stairs. And that which shall most weigh your shoulders down will be the evil and senseless company with which you shall fall into this vale; which shall then become all ungrateful, all mad and malevolent against you, but, soon after, their brows, not yours, shall redden for it. Of their brutish folly their own conduct shall afford the proof, so that it will be for your fair fame to have made you a party by yourself.

'Your first refuge and first inn shall be the courtesy of the great Lombard who bears the holy bird upon the ladder, and he will have for you such benign regard that, in doing and in asking, between you two, that will be first which between others is the slowest. With him you shall see one who, at his birth, was so stamped by this strong star, that notable shall be his deeds. Not yet have folk taken due note of him, because of his young age, for these wheels have revolved around him only nine years; but before the Gascon deceives the lofty Henry, some sparks of his virtue shall appear, in his caring naught for money or for toils. His magnificence shall hereafter be so known, that his very foes will not be able to keep silent tongues about him. Look you to him and to his benefits. By him shall many folk be changed, the rich and the beggarly altering their condition. And you shall bear hence written of him in your mind, but you shall not tell it'; — and he told things past the belief even of those who shall see them. Then he added, 'Son, these are the glosses on what was said to you: behold the snares which are hidden behind but a few circlings. Yet I would not have you envious of your neighbors, since your life shall be prolonged far beyond the punishment of their perfidies.'

When by his silence the holy soul showed he had finished setting the woof across the warp I had held out in readiness to him, I began, as he who, in doubt, craves counsel of one who sees and rightly wills and loves, 'I see well, my father, how time spurs toward me to give me such a blow as is heaviest to whosoever is most heedless; wherefore it is good that I arm myself with foresight, so that if the dearest place be taken from me, I lose not all the rest by reason of my songs. Down in the world endlessly bitter, and upon the mountain from whose fair summit my lady's eyes uplifted me, and after, through the heavens from light to light, I have learned that which, if I tell again, will have for many a savor of great bitterness; and if I am a timid friend to the truth, I fear to lose life among those who shall call this time ancient.'

The light wherein was smiling the treasure I had found there first became flashing as a golden mirror in the sun, then it replied, 'A conscience dark, either with its own or with another's shame, will indeed feel your speech to be harsh. But none the less, all falsehood set aside, make manifest all that you have seen; and then let them scratch where the itch is. For if at first taste your voice be grievous, yet shall it leave thereafter vital nourishment when digested. This cry of yours shall do as does the wind, which smites most upon the loftiest summits; and this shall be no little cause of honor.

Therefore only the souls known of fame have been shown to you within these wheels, upon the mountain, and in the woeful valley; for the mind of him who hears rests not nor confirms its faith by an example that has its roots unknown or hidden, nor for other proof that is not manifest.'

CANTO XVIII

ALREADY THAT blessed mirror was enjoying only its own thoughts, and I was tasting mine, tempering the bitter with the sweet, when the lady who was leading me to God said, 'Change your thought: consider that I am in His presence who lightens the burden of every wrong.'

I turned round at the loving sound of my Comfort, and what love I then saw in the holy eyes I leave here untold; not only because I distrust my own speech, but because of memory, which cannot return on itself so far unless Another guide it. This much of that moment can I retell, that as I gazed upon her my affection was freed from every other desire so long as the Eternal Joy that shone direct on Beatrice satisfied me from the fair eyes with its reflected aspect. Overcoming me with the light of a smile, she said to me, 'Turn and listen, for not only in my eyes is Paradise.'

As sometimes here the affection is seen in the countenance if it be such that all the mind is taken up by it, so in the flaming of the holy glow to which I turned I recognized his wish to have some further speech with me; and he began, 'In this fifth tier of the tree, which has life from its top and is always in fruit and never sheds its leaves, are blessed spirits which below, before they came to heaven, were of such great renown that every Muse would be rich with them. Look, therefore, upon the horns of the cross: he whom I shall name there will do as in a cloud its swift fire does.'

At the naming of Joshua, even as it was done, I saw a light drawn along the cross, nor was the word noted by me before the fact; and at the name of the great Maccabeus I saw another move, wheeling, and gladness was the whip of the top. So for Charlemagne and Roland my intent gaze followed two of them, as the eye follows its falcon and he flies; next William, and Renouard and Duke Godfrey drew my sight along that cross, and Robert Guiscard too. Then, moving and mingling among the other lights, the soul which had spoken with me showed me how great an artist it was among the singers of that heaven.

I turned to my right side, to see in Beatrice my duty, signified either by speech or by gesture, and I saw her eyes so clear, so joyful, that her aspect surpassed all it had been at other times, even the last. And as from feeling more delight in doing well, a man from day to day becomes aware that his virtue makes advance, so did I perceive that my circling round with the heaven had increased its arc, when I saw that miracle even more adorned. And such change as comes in a moment over the face of a pale lady, when her countenance frees itself from a burden of modest shame, was presented to my eyes when I turned, because of the whiteness of the temperate sixth star which had received me within itself.

I saw in that torch of Jove the sparkling of the love that was there, trace out our speech to my eyes; and as birds, risen from the shore, as if rejoicing together at their pasture, make of themselves now a round flock, now some other shape, so within the lights holy creatures were singing as they flew, and in their figures made of themselves now *D*, now *I*, now *L*. At first, as they sang, they moved to their own notes; then, as they became one of these characters, they stopped a little and were silent.

O divine Pegasea, who give glory unto men of genius and render them long-lived, as they, through you, the cites and the kingdoms, illumine me with yourself that I may set forth their shapes, as I have them in conception; let your power appear in these brief lines.

They displayed themselves then, in five times seven vowels and consonants; and I took note of the parts as they appeared in utterance to me. DILIGITE IUSTITIAM were the first verb and substantive of all the design; QUI IUDICA-TIS TERRAM were the last. Then, ordered in the *M* of the fifth word they stayed, so that Jove seemed silver in that place, pricked out with gold; and I saw other lights descending where the top of the *M* was, and become quiet there,

singing, I believe, the Good that draws them to Itself. Then, as on the striking of burning logs there rise innumerable sparks, wherefrom the foolish are wont to draw auguries, so thence there seemed to rise again more than a thousand lights, and mount, some much, some little, even as the Sun which kindles them allotted them; and when each had rested in its place, I saw the head and the neck of an eagle represented by that patterned fire. He who there paints has none to guide Him, but He Himself does guide, and from Him is recognized that virtue which shapes nests. The rest of the blessed spirits, which at first seemed content to form a lily on the *M*, with a slight motion completed the design.

O sweet star, how many and how bright were the gems which made it plain to me that our justice is the effect of the heaven which you engem! Wherefore I pray the Mind, in which your motion and your virtue have their beginning, that It look on the place whence issues the smoke that dims your radiance, so that once again It may be wroth at the buying and the selling in the temple which made its walls of miracles and martyrdoms. O soldiery of Heaven whom I look upon, pray for all those who have gone astray on earth, following the ill example. Of old it was the wont to make war with swords, but now it is made by taking away, now here now there, the bread which the tender Father bars from none.

But you that write only to cancel, bethink you that Peter and Paul, who died for the vineyard that you are laying waste, are still alive. Though you indeed may say, 'I have my desire so set on him who willed to live alone, and who, for a dance, was dragged to martyrdom, that I know not the Fisherman nor Paul.'

Canto XIX

WITH OUTSTRETCHED wings appeared before me the beautiful image which those interwoven souls, joyful in their sweet fruition, were making. Each of them seemed a little ruby on which a ray of sun should glow so enkindled as to reflect it into my eyes. And that which I must now tell, never did voice report

nor ink record, nor was it ever comprised by phantasy; for I saw and also heard the beak speaking, and uttering with its voice *I* and *Mine* when in conception it was *We* and *Our*. And it began, 'For being just and duteous am I here exalted to that glory which cannot be surpassed by desire; and upon earth have I left such a memory that the wicked people there commend it, but follow not its story.' Thus one sole heat makes itself felt from many embers, even as from many loves one sole sound issued from that image.

And I then, 'O perpetual flowers of the eternal bliss, who make all your odors seem to me but one, breathe forth and deliver me from the great fast which has long held me hunger-ing, not finding any food for it on earth. Well do I know that if the Divine Justice makes another realm in heaven Its mirror, yours does not apprehend It through a veil. You know how eager I prepare myself to listen; you know what is that question which is so old a fast to me.'

As the falcon which, issuing from the hood, moves his head and flaps his wings, showing his will and making himself fine, such did I see that ensign which was woven of praises of the Divine Grace become, with songs such as he knows who thereabove rejoices. Then it began, 'He that turned His compass round the limit of the world, and within it marked out so much both hidden and revealed, could not so imprint His power on all the universe that His word should not remain in infinite excess; and this is certified by that first proud one, who was the highest of all creatures and who, through not awaiting light, fell unripe; from which it is plain that every lesser nature is too scant a vessel for that Good which has not limit and measures Itself by Itself. Thus your vision, which must needs be one of the rays of the Mind with which all things are replete, cannot of its own nature be of such power that it should not perceive its origin to be far beyond all that is apparent to it. Therefore the sight that is granted to your world penetrates within the Eternal Justice as the eye into the sea; which, though from the shore it can see the bottom, in the open sea it sees it not, and none the less it is there, but the depth conceals it. There is no light unless it comes from that serene which is never clouded, else is it darkness, either shadow of the flesh or its poison.

'Now is laid well open to you the hiding-place which concealed from you the living Justice concerning which you have made question so incessantly. For you said, 'A man is born on the bank of the Indus, and none is there to speak, or read, or write, of Christ, and all his wishes and acts are good, so far as human reason sees, without sin in life or in speech. He dies unbaptized, and without faith. Where is this justice which condemns him? Where is his sin if he does not believe?' Now who are you who would sit upon the seat to judge at a thousand miles away with the short sight that carries but a span? Assuredly, for him who subtilizes with me, if the Scriptures were not set over you, there would be marvelous occasion for questioning. O earthly animals! O gross minds! The primal Will, which of Itself is good, has never moved from Itself, which is the supreme Good. All is just that accords with It; no created good draws It to itself, but It, raying forth, is the cause of it.'

As the stork circles over her nest, when she has fed her young, and as the one which she has fed looks up to her, such became (and I so raised my brows) the blessed image which, impelled by so many counsels, moved its wings. Wheeling it sang and said, 'As are my notes to you who understand them not, such is the Eternal Judgment to you mortals.'

After those glowing flames of the Holy Spirit became quiet, still in the sign which made the Romans reverend to the world, it began again, 'To this realm none ever rose who believed not in Christ, either before or after he was nailed to the tree. But behold, many cry Christ, Christ, who, at the Judgment, shall be far less near to Him than he who knows not Christ; and the Ethiop will condemn such Christians when the two companies shall be separated, the one forever rich, and the other poor. What may the Persians say to your kings, when they shall see that volume open in which are recorded all their dispraises? There shall be seen, among the deeds of Albert, that which will soon set the pen in motion, by which the Kingdom of Prague shall be made a desert.

There shall be seen the woe which he who shall die by a boarskin blow is bringing upon the Seine by falsifying the coin. There shall be seen the pride that quickens thirst, which makes the Scot and the Englishman mad, so that neither can keep within his own bounds. It will show the lechery and effeminate life of him of Spain, and him of Bohemia, who never knew valor nor wished it. It will show the Cripple of Jerusalem, his goodness marked with an *I*, while an *M* will mark the opposite. It will show the avarice and cowardice of him who has in ward the Isle of Fire where Anchises ended his long life; and to give to understand how paltry he is, the writing for him shall be in contractions that will note much in little space. And plain to all shall be revealed the foul deeds of his uncle and his brother, which have dishonored so eminent a lineage and two crowns. And he of Portugal and he of Norway shall be known there, and he of Rascia, who, to his harm, has seen the coin of Venice.

'O happy Hungary, if she no longer allow herself to be maltreated! and happy Navarre, if she arm herself with the mountains which bind her round! And all should believe that, for earnest of this, Nicosia and Famagosta are now lamenting and complaining because of their beast who departs not from the side of the others.'

CANTO XX

WHEN HE who illumines all the world descends from our hemisphere so that day on every side is spent, the heaven, which before is kindled by him alone, suddenly shows itself again with many lights wherein one alone is shining; and this change in the sky came to my mind when the ensign of the world and of its leaders became silent in the blessed beak; because all those living lights, shining far more brightly, began songs that have lapsed and fallen from my memory.

O sweet Love, that mantlest thyself in a smile, how glowing didst thou appear in those pipes that were filled only with the breath of holy thoughts!

When the bright and precious jewels wherewith I saw the sixth luminary engemmed had imposed silence on these angelic chimes, I seemed to hear the murmuring of a river which falls down clear from rock to rock, showing the abundance of its high source. And as the sound takes its form at the neck of the lute, and the wind at the vent of the pipe it fills, so, without keeping me waiting longer, that murmuring of the Eagle rose up through the neck, as if it were hollow. There it became voice, and thence it issued through the beak in the form of words such as the heart whereon I wrote them was awaiting.

'That part in me which in mortal eagles sees and endures the sun you must now gaze on intently,' it began to me, 'because, of the fires whereof I make my shape, those with which the eye in my head is sparkling are of all their ranks the chiefs. He that shines midmost, as the pupil, was the singer of the Holy Ghost, who bore the ark about from town to town. Now he knows the merit of his song, so far as it was the effect of his own counsel, by the reward which is proportioned to it. Of the five which make an arch for my brow, he who is nearest to my beak consoled the poor widow for her son. Now he knows, by experience of this sweet life and of the opposite, how dear it costs not to follow Christ. And he who follows on the circumfer-ence whereof I speak, upon the upward arc, by true penitence delayed death. Now he knows that the eternal judgment is not changed when worthy prayer there below makes tomorrow's that which was today's. The next who follows, with a good intention which bore bad fruit, made himself Greek, together with the laws and me, in order to give place to the Pastor. Now he knows how the evil derived from his good action does not harm him, even though the world should be destroyed thereby. And him you see in the downward arc was William, for whom that land mourns that weeps on account of the living Charles and Frederick. Now he knows how Heaven is enamored of the righteous king, as by the effulgence of his aspect he yet makes this evident. Who would believe, down in the erring world, that Ripheus the Trojan was the fifth of the holy lights in this circle? Now he knows much of the divine grace that the world cannot see, even though his sight discerns not the bottom.'

Like the lark that soars in the air, first singing, then silent, content with the last sweetness that satiates it, so seemed to me the image of the imprint of the Eternal Pleasure, by whose will everything becomes that which it is. And albeit there I was to my questioning like glass to the color that it clothes, yet would it not endure to bide its time in silence, but by its weight and pressure forced from my lips, 'How can these things be?' At which I saw a great festival of flashing lights. And then, its eye kindling yet more, the blessed sign, not to keep me in suspense and amazement, replied, 'I see that you believe these things because I tell them, but you see not the *how*, so that, though believed in, they are hidden. You do as one who well apprehends a thing by name, but may not see its quiddity unless another explain it. *Regnum celorum* suffers violence from fervent love and from living hope which vanquishes the Divine will: not as man overcomes man, but vanquishes it because it wills to be vanquished, and vanquished, vanquishes with its own benignity. The first soul of the eyebrow and the fifth make you marvel, because you see the region of the Angels decked with them. They came forth from their bodies not as you think, Gentiles, but Christians, with firm faith, the one in the Feet that were to suffer, the other in the Feet that had suffered. For the one came back to his bones from Hell, where none ever returns to right will; and this was the reward of living hope, of living hope that gave power to the prayers made to God to raise him up, that it might be possible for his will to be moved. The glorious soul I tell of, having returned to the flesh for a short time, believed in Him that was able to help him; and, believing, was kindled to such a fire of true love that on his second death he was worthy to come to this rejoicing. The other, through grace that wells from a fountain so deep that never did creature thrust eye down to its first wave, set all his love below on righteousness; wherefore, from grace to grace, God opened his eye to our future redemption, so that he believed in it, and thenceforth endured not the stench of paganism, and reproved the perverse peoples for it. Those three ladies whom you saw by the right wheel

stood for baptism to him more than a thousand years before baptizing.

'O predestination, how remote is thy root from the vision of those who see not the First Cause entire! And you mortals, keep yourselves restrained in judging; for we, who see God, know not yet all the elect. And to us such defect is sweet, because our good in this good is refined, that what God wills we also will.'

Thus, to make my short sight clear, sweet medicine was given to me by that divine image. And as a good lutanist makes the vibration of the string accompany a good singer, by which the song gains more pleasantness, so, I remember that, while it spoke, I saw the two blessed lights, just as the winking of the eyes concords, making their flames quiver to the words.

Canto XXI

ALREADY MY eyes were fixed again on the face of my lady, and with them in mind, and from every other intent it was withdrawn; and she did not smile, but, 'Were I to smile,' she began to me, 'you would become such as was Semele when she turned to ashes; for my beauty which, along the steps of the eternal palace, is kindled the more, as you have seen, the higher the ascent, were it not tempered, is so resplendent that your mortal powers at its flash would be like the bough shattered by a thunderbolt. We have risen to the seventh splendor which beneath the breast of the burning Lion rays down now mingled with its power. Fix your mind after your eyes, and make of them mirrors to the figure which in this mirror shall be shown to you.'

He who should know what was the pasture of my sight in her blessed aspect, when I transferred me to another care, would recognize how much it rejoiced me to be obedient to my heavenly guide, weighing the one with the other side.

Within the crystal which bears the name, circling round the world, of its beloved leader beneath whom every wickedness lay dead, I saw, of the color of gold on which a sunbeam is shining, a ladder rising up so high that my sight might not follow it. I saw, moreover, so many splendors descending along the steps, that I

thought every light which appears in heaven had been poured down from it.

And, as by their natural custom, the daws move about together, at the beginning of the day, to warm their cold feathers, then some fly away not to return, some wheel round to whence they had started, while others wheeling make a stay; such movements, it seemed to me, were in that sparkling, which came in a throng, as soon as it smote upon a certain step.

And that one which stopped nearest to us became so bright that in my thought I said, 'I clearly perceive the love which you are signaling to me. But she from whom I await the how and the when of speech and of silence pauses, and therefore I, counter to desire, do well not to ask.' Whereupon she, who saw my silence in His sight who sees all, said to me, 'Loose your warm desire.' And I began, 'My own merit does not make me worthy of your answer, but for her sake who gives me leave to ask, O blessed life that are hidden within your own joy, make known to me the cause that has placed you so near me; and tell why in this wheel the sweet symphony of Paradise is silent, which below through the others so devoutly sounds.'

'You have the hearing as the sight of mortals,' it replied to me, 'wherefore here is no song, for that same reason for which Beatrice has not smiled. Down by the steps of the sacred ladder I descended so far only to give you glad welcome with my speech and with the light that mantles me; nor was it greater love that made me swifter; for love as much and more is burning up there, even as the flaming manifests to you; but the high charity which makes us prompt servants of the counsel which governs the world allots here as you perceive.'

'I see well,' said I, 'O holy lamp, how free love suffices in this Court for following the eternal Providence; but this is what seems to me hard to discern, why you alone among your consorts were predestined to this office.' Nor had I come to the last word when the light made a center of its middle, and spun round like a rapid millstone. Then answered the love that was therein, 'A divine light is directed on me, penetrating through this wherein I embosom myself, the virtue of which, conjoined with my vision, lifts me above myself so far that I see the Supreme Essence from which it is drawn. From this comes the joy with which I am aflame, for to my sight, in the measure of its clearness, I match the clearness of my flame. But that soul in heaven which is most enlightened, that Seraph who has his eye most fixed on God, could not satisfy your question; for that which you ask lies so deep within the abyss of the eternal statute that it is cut off from every created vision. And when you return to the mortal world, carry this back, so that it may no longer presume to move its feet toward so great a goal. The mind, which shines here, on earth is smoky, and therefore think how it can do below that which it cannot do, though heaven raise it to itself.'

His words so restrained me that I left the question and drew me back to ask it humbly who it was. 'Between the two shores of Italy, and not very far from your native land, rise crags so high that the thunders sound far lower down; and they make a hump whose name is Catria, beneath which a hermitage is consecrated, which once was wholly given to worship.' Thus it began again to me with its third speech; then continued, 'There in the service of God I became so steadfast that with food seasoned only with olive-juice I passed easily through heats and frosts, content in contemplative thoughts. That cloister used to yield abundant harvest to these heavens, and now it is become so barren that soon it needs must be revealed. In that place was I Peter Damian, and in the House of Our Lady on the Adriatic shore I was Peter the Sinner. Little of mortal life was left to me when I was sought for and dragged to that hat which ever passes down from bad to worse. Cephas came, and the great vessel of the Holy Spirit came, lean and barefoot, taking their food at whatsoever inn. Now the modern pastors require one to prop them upon this side and one on that, and one to lead them, so heavy are they, and one to hold up their mantles, so that two beasts go under one hide. O patience, that do endure so much!'

At these words I saw more flamelets from step to step descending, and whirling; and every whirl made them more beautiful. Round about this one they came, and stopped, and uttered a cry of such deep sound that nothing here could be likened to it; nor did I understand it, so did the thunder overcome me.

CANTO XXII

OVERWHELMED WITH amazement, I turned to my guide, like a little child who always runs back to where it has most confidence; and she, like a mother who quickly comforts her pale and gasping son with her voice which is wont to reassure him, said to me, 'Do you not know that you are in heaven, do you not know that heaven is all holy, and that whatever is done here comes of righteous zeal? How the song, and I by smiling, would have transmuted you, you can now conceive, since this cry has so much moved you; wherein, had you understood their prayers, already would be known to you the vengeance which you shall see before you die. The sword of here on high cuts not in haste nor tardily, save to his deeming who in longing or in fear awaits it. But turn now to the others, for you shall see many illustrious spirits, if you direct your sight as I say.'

As was her pleasure, I turned my eyes, and I saw a hundred little spheres which together were making themselves beautiful with their mutual rays. I was standing as one who within himself represses the prick of his desire, who does not make bold to ask, he so fears to exceed. And the greatest and most shining of those pearls came forward to satisfy my desire concerning itself. Then within it I heard, 'If you could see, as I do, the charity which burns among us, you would have uttered your thoughts; but lest you, by waiting, be delayed in your lofty aim, I will make answer to the thought itself about which you are so circumspect.

'That mountain on whose slope Cassino lies was of old frequented on its summit by the folk deceived and perverse, and I am he who first bore up there His name who brought to earth that truth which so uplifts us; and such grace shone upon me that I drew away the surrounding towns from the impious worship that seduced the world. These other fires were all contemplative men, kindled by that warmth which gives birth to holy flowers and fruits. Here is Macarius, here is Romualdus, here are my brethren who stayed their feet within the cloisters and kept a steadfast heart.'

And I to him, 'The affection you show in speaking with me, and the good semblance which I see and note in all your ardors, have expanded my confidence as the sun does the rose when it opens to its fullest bloom. Therefore I pray you — and do you, father, assure me if I am capable of receiving, so great a grace, that I may behold you in your uncovered shape.'

Whereon he, 'Brother, your high desire shall be fulfilled up in the last sphere, where are fulfilled all others and my own. There every desire is perfect, mature, and whole. In that alone is every part there where it always was, for it is not in space, nor has it poles; and our ladder reaches up to it, wherefore it steals itself from your sight. All the way thither the patriarch Jacob saw it stretch its upper part, when it appeared to him so laden with Angels. But no one now lifts his foot from earth to ascend it, and my Rule remains for waste of paper. The walls, which used to be an abbey, have become dens, and the cowls are sacks full of foul meal. But heavy usury is not exacted so counter to God's pleasure as that fruit which makes the heart of monks so mad; for whatsoever the Church has in keeping is all for the folk that ask it in God's name, not for kindred, or for other filthier thing. The flesh of mortals is so soft that on earth a good beginning does not last from the springing of the oak to the bearing of the acorn. Peter began his fellowship without gold or silver, and I mine with prayer and with fasting, and Francis his with humility; and if you look at the beginning of each, and then look again whither it has strayed, you will see the white changed to dark. Nevertheless, Jordan driven back, and the sea fleeing when God willed, were sights more wondrous than the succor here.'

Thus he spoke to me, then drew back to his company, and the company closed together; then like a whirlwind all were gathered upward. My sweet lady, with only a sign, thrust me up after them by that ladder, so did her power overcome my nature; nor ever here below, where we mount and descend by nature's law, was motion so swift as might match my flight. So may I return, reader, to that devout triumph for the sake of which I often bewail my sins and beat my breast, you would not have drawn out and put your finger into the fire so quickly as I saw the sign which follows the Bull, and was within it.

O glorious stars, O light impregnated with mighty power, from which I derive all my genius, whatsoever it may be, with you was rising and with you was hiding himself he who is father of every mortal life when I first felt the air of Tuscany; and then, when the grace was bestowed on me to enter the lofty wheel that bears you round, your region was assigned to me! To you my soul now devoutly sighs, that it may acquire virtue for the hard pass which draws it to itself.

'You are so near to the final blessedness,' Beatrice began, 'that you must have your eyes clear and keen. And therefore, before you enter farther into it, look back downward and behold how great a world I have already set beneath your feet, in order that your heart may present itself, joyous to its utmost, to the triumphant throng which comes glad through this round ether.'

With my sight I returned through all and each of the seven spheres, and saw this globe such that I smiled at its paltry semblance; and that counsel I approve as best which holds it for least, and he whose thought is turned elsewhere may be called truly upright. I saw the daughter of Latona glowing without that shade for which I once believed her rare and dense. The aspect of your son, Hyperion, I there endured, and saw how Maia and Dione move around and near him. Then appeared to me the tempering of Jove between his father and his son, and then was clear to me the varying they make in their position. And all the seven were displayed to me, how great they are and swift, and how distant each from other in location. The little threshing-floor which makes us so fierce was all revealed to me from hills to river-mouths, as I circled with the eternal Twins. Then to the beauteous eyes I turned my eyes again.

CANTO XXIII

As the bird, among the beloved leaves, having sat on the nest of her sweet brood through the night which hides things from us, who, in order to look upon their longed-for aspect and to find the food wherewith to feed them, wherein her heavy toils are pleasing to her, foreruns the time, upon the open bough, and with glowing love awaits the sun, fixedly gazing for the dawn to break; so was my lady standing, erect and eager, turned toward the region beneath which the sun shows less haste. I, therefore, seeing her in suspense and longing, became as he who in desire would fain have something else, and in hope is satisfied. But short was the time between the one and the other *when*, of my waiting, I mean, and of my seeing the heavens become more and more resplendent. And Beatrice said, 'Behold the hosts of Christ's triumph and all the fruit garnered from the circling of these spheres!' It seemed to me her face was all aflame, and her eyes were so full of joy that I must needs pass it by undescribed.

As in the clear skies at the full moon Trivia smiles among the eternal nymphs that deck heaven through all its depths, I saw, above thousands of lamps, a Sun which kindled each one of them as does our own the things we see above; and through its living light the lucent Substance outglowed so bright upon my vision that it endured it not.

O Beatrice, sweet guide and dear! She said to me, 'That which overcomes you is power against which naught defends itself. Therein are the wisdom and the power that opened the roads between Heaven and earth, for which of old there was such long desire.'

Even as fire breaks from a cloud, because it dilates so that it has not room there, and contrary to its own nature, falls down to earth, so my mind, becoming greater amid those feasts, issued from itself, and of what it became has no remembrance.

'Open your eyes and look on what I am; you have seen things such that you are become able to sustain my smile.' I was as one that wakes from a forgotten dream, and who strives in vain

to bring it back to mind, when I heard this proffer, worthy of such gratitude that it can never be effaced from the book which records the past.

Though all those tongues which Polyhymnia and her sisters made most rich with their sweetest milk should sound now to aid me, it would not come to a thousandth part of the truth, in singing the holy smile, and how it lit up the holy aspect; and so, depicting Paradise, the sacred poem must needs make a leap, even as one who finds his way cut off. But whoso thinks of the ponderous theme and of the mortal shoulder which is laden therewith, will not blame it if it tremble beneath the load. It is no voyage for a little bark, this which my daring prow cleaves as it goes, nor for a pilot who would spare himself.

'Why does my face so enamor you that you turn not to the fair garden which blossoms beneath the rays of Christ? Here is the Rose wherein the Divine World became flesh; here are the lilies by whose odor the good way was taken.'

Thus Beatrice; and I who to her counsels was all eager, again gave myself up to the battle of the feeble brows.

As under the sun's ray, which streams pure through a broken cloud, ere now my eyes, sheltered by shade, have seen a meadow of flowers, so saw I many hosts of splendors glowed on from above by ardent rays, though I saw not whence came the glowings. O benign Power, which doth so imprint them, Thou didst ascend so as to yield place there for the eyes that were powerless before Thee!

The name of the flair flower which I ever invoke, both morning and evening, absorbed all my mind as I gazed on the greatest flame. And when on both of my eyes had been depicted the quality and the greatness of the living star which conquers up there even as down here it conquered, there descended through the heaven a torch which formed a circle in the likeness of a crown that girt her and wheeled about her. Whatever melody sounds sweetest here below and most draws to itself the soul, would seem a cloud which, being rent, thunders, compared with the sound of that lyre wherewith was crowned the beauteous sapphire by which the brightest heaven is ensapphired.

'I am angelic love, who circle the supreme joy that breathes from out the womb which was the hostelry of our Desire; and I shall circle, Lady of Heaven, until thou shalt follow thy Son, and make the supreme sphere more divine by entering it.' Thus the circling melody sealed itself, and all the other lights made Mary's name resound.

The royal mantle of all the world's revolving spheres, which most burns and is most quickened in the breath of God and in His workings, had, above us, its inner shore so distant that sight of it, there where I was, was not yet possible to me. Therefore my eyes had not power to follow the crowned flame which mounted upward after her offspring. And as an infant which, when it has taken the milk, stretches its arms toward its mother, its affection glowing forth, each of these splendors stretched upward with its peak, so that the deep love they had for Mary was made plain to me. Then they remained there in my sight, singing *Regina celi* so sweetly that never has the delight departed from me. Oh, how great is the abundance which is heaped up in those rich coffers, who were good sowers here below! Here they live and rejoice in the treasure which was gained with tears in the exile of Babylon, where gold was scorned. Here, under the exalted Son of God and Mary, together with both the ancient and the new council, he triumphs in his victory who holds the keys of such glory.

CANTO XXIV

'O FELLOWSHIP elect to the great supper of the blessed Lamb, who feeds you so that your desire is ever satisfied, since by the grace of God this man foretastes of that which falls from your table before death appoint his time to him, give heed to his immense longing and bedew him somewhat: you drink ever of the fountain whence flows that which he thinks.' Thus Beatrice; and those glad souls made themselves spheres upon fixed poles, flaming like comets, as they whirled. And as wheels within the fittings of clocks revolve, so

that to one who gives heed the first seems quiet and the last to fly, so did those carols, dancing severally fast and slow, make me judge of their riches. From the one I noted as the richest I saw issue a fire so joyful that it left there none of greater brightness; and it revolved three times round Beatrice with a song so divine that my phantasy does not repeat it to me; wherefore my pen leaps and I do not write it, for our imagination, not to say our speech, is of too vivid color for such folds.

'O holy sister mine, who do so devoutly pray to us, by your ardent affection you loose me from that fair sphere'; after it had stopped, the blessed fire breathed forth these words to my lady as I have told them.

And she, 'O eternal light of the great man with whom our Lord left the keys, which He bore below, of this marvelous joy, test this man on points light and grave, as pleases you, concerning the Faith by which you did walk upon the sea. Whether he loves rightly and rightly hopes and believes is not hidden from you, for you have your vision where everything is seen depicted. But since this kingdom has made its citizens by the true faith, it rightly falls to him to speak of it, that he may glorify it.'

Even as the bachelor arms himself — and does not speak until the master propounds the question — in order to adduce the proof, not to decide it, so, while she was speaking, I was arming myself with every reason, to be ready for such a questioner and for such a profession.

'Speak, good Christian, and declare yourself: Faith, what is it?' Whereon I raised my brow to that light whence this was breathed forth, then I turned to Beatrice, who promptly signaled to me that I should pour the water forth from my inward fountain.

'May the grace that grants me to confess to the Chief Centurion,' I began, 'cause my conceptions to be well expressed.' And I went on, 'As the veracious pen of your dear brother wrote of it, who with you, father, put Rome on the good path, Faith is the substance of things hoped for and the evidence of things not seen; and this I take to be its quiddity.'

Then I heard, 'Rightly do you deem, if you understand well why he placed it among the substances and then among the evidences.'

And I thereon, 'The deep things which grant to me here the sight of themselves are so hidden to eyes below that there their existence is in belief alone, upon which the lofty hope is founded; and therefore it takes the designation of substance. And from this belief needs must we reason, without seeing more: therefore it receives the designation of evidence.' Then I heard, 'If all that is acquired below for doctrine were thus understood, the wit of sophist would have no place there.' These words were breathed forth from that enkindled love; and it continued, 'Now the alloy and the weight of this coin have been well enough examined; but tell me if you have it in your purse?' And I, 'Yes, I have it so shining and so round that in its stamp nothing is doubtful to me.'

Then issued from the deep light that was shining there, 'This precious jewel whereon every virtue is founded, whence did it come to you?'

And I, 'The plenteous rain of the Holy Spirit which is poured over the old and over the new parchments is a syllogism that has proved it to me so acutely that, in comparison with this, every demonstration seems obtuse to me.'

Then I heard, 'That old and that new proposition which are so conclusive to you why do you hold them for divine discourse?'

And I, 'The proof which discloses the truth to me are the works that followed, for which nature never heats iron nor beats anvil.'

'Tell me,' came the reply, 'who assures you that these works ever were? The very thing itself which requires to be proved, and naught else, affirms them to you.'

'If the world turned to Christianity without miracles,' I said, 'that one is such that the rest are not the hundredth part; for you entered the field poor and hungry, to sow the good plant which was once a vine and is now become a thorn.'

This ended, the high and holy court resounded a '*Te Deum laudamus*' through the spheres, in the melody which up there is sung.

And that Baron who, thus from branch to branch examining, had now drawn me on so that we were approaching the last leaves, began again, 'The Grace that holds amorous discourse with your mind, till now has opened your lips aright, so that I approve what has come from them; but now you must declare what you believe and whence it was offered to your belief.'

'O holy father, spirit who see that which you did so believe that you, toward the sepulchre, did outdo younger feet,' I began, 'you would have me declare here the form of my ready belief, and also you have asked the cause of it. And I reply: I believe in one God, sole and eternal, who, unmoved, moves all the heavens with love and with desire; and for this belief I have not only proofs physical and metaphysical, but it is given to me also in the truth that rains down hence through Moses and the Prophets and the Psalms, through the Gospel, and through you who wrote when the fiery Spirit had made you holy. And I believe in three Eternal Persons, and these I believe to be one essence, so one and so threefold as to comport at once with *are* and *is*. With the profound divine state whereof I now speak, the evangelic doctrine many times sets the seal upon my mind. This is the beginning, this is the spark which then dilates to a living flame and like a star in heaven shines within me.'

Even as the master who listens to that which pleases him, then embraces his servant, rejoicing in his news, as soon as he is silent; so, singing benedictions on me, the apostolic light at whose bidding I had spoken encircled me three times when I was silent, I so pleased him by my speech.

CANTO XXV

IF EVER it come to pass that the sacred poem to which heaven and earth have so set hand that it has made me lean for many years should overcome the cruelty which bars me from the fair sheepfold where I slept as a lamb, an enemy to the wolves which war on it, with changed voice now and with changed fleece a poet will I return, and at the font of my baptism will I take the crown; because there I entered into the Faith that makes souls known to God; and afterward Peter, for its sake, thus encircled my brow.

Then a light moved towards us from that circle whence had issued the first-fruit which

Christ left of His vicars; and my lady, full of gladness, said to me, 'Look! look! Behold the Baron for whose sake, down below, folk visit Galicia.'

As when the dove alights beside its mate, and the one lavishes its affection on the other, circling it and cooing, so did I see the one great and glorious prince received by the other, praising the food which feeds them thereabove. But when the joyful greeting was completed, each stopped silent *coram me*, so aflame that it overcame my sight. Then Beatrice, smiling, said, 'Illustrious life, by whom the bounty of our Court was chronicled, make hope resound in this height; you can, who did figure it all those times when Jesus showed most favor to the three.'

'Lift up your head and see that you reassure yourself, for that which comes up here from the mortal world must be ripened in our beams.' This assurance came to me from the second fire; whereon I lifted up my eyes unto the hills which had bent them down before with excess of weight.

'Since, of His grace, our Emperor wills that you, before your death, come face to face with His Counts in His most secret hall, so that, having seen the truth of this Court, you may strengthen in yourself and others the Hope which there below rightly enamors, say what it is, and how your mind blossoms with it, and say whence it came to you.' Thus the second light continued further.

And that compassionate one, who had guided the feathers of my wings to such lofty flight, anticipated my reply thus, 'The Church Militant has not any child possessed of more hope, as is written in the Sun which irradiates all our host; therefore is it granted him to come from Egypt to Jerusalem, that he may see, before his term of warfare is completed. The other two points which are asked, not for sake of knowing, but that he may report how greatly this virtue is pleasing to you, I leave to him, for they will not be difficult to him, nor of vainglory; and let him answer thereto, and may the grace of God concede this to him.'

As the pupil who answers the teacher, ready and eager in that wherein he is expert, so that his worth may be disclosed, 'Hope,' I said, 'is a

sure expectation of future glory, which divine grace produces, and preceding merit. From many stars this light comes to me, but he first instilled it into my heart who was the supreme singer of the Supreme Leader. 'Let them hope in Thee who know Thy name,' he says in his divine song, and who knows it not, if he have my faith. You afterwards in your Epistle did instill it into me, together with his instilling, so that I am full, and pour again your shower upon others.'

While I was speaking, within the living bosom of that fire trembled a flash, sudden and frequent, like lightning; then it breathed forth, 'The love whereof I am still aflame toward that virtue which followed me even to the palm and the departure from the field wills that I breathe again to you, who do delight in it; and it is my pleasure that you tell that which Hope promises to you.'

And I, 'The new and the old Scriptures set up the token of the souls that God has made His friends, and this points it out to me. Isaiah says that each one shall be clothed in his own land with a double garment, and his own land is this sweet life; and your brother, where he treats of the white robes, makes manifest this revelation to us far more expressly.'

At first, close on the end of these words, '*Sperent in te*' was heard above us, to which all the carols made answer; then one light among them shone out so bright that if the Crab had one such crystal, winter would have a month of one unbroken day. And as a glad maiden rises and goes and enters into the dance, only to do honor to the bride, not for any failing, so did I see the brightened splendor approach the two who were wheeling to such a song as befitted their burning love. It joined there in the singing and the wheeling, and my lady kept her gaze upon them, even as a bride silent and motionless. 'This is he who lay upon the breast of our Pelican, and this is he who was chosen from upon the Cross for the great office.' Thus my lady; but no more after than before her words did she move after than before her words did she move her gaze from its fixed attention.

As is he who gazes and strains to see the sun a little eclipsed, and who through seeing becomes sightless, so did I become in respect to that last fire, till it was said, 'Why do you dazzle yourself in order to see that which has here no place? On earth my body is earth, and there it shall be with the rest, until our number equals the eternal purpose. With the two robes in the blessed cloister and those two lights only which ascended; and this you shall carry back into your world.'

At these words the flaming circle fell silent, together with the sweet mingling made within the sound of the trinal breath, even as, to avoid fatigue or danger, oars till then struck through the water, stop all at once at the sound of a whistle.

Ah! how greatly was I stirred in my mind when I turned to see Beatrice, at not being able to see, although I was near her, and in the world of bliss.

CANTO XXVI

WHILE I WAS apprehensive because of my quenched sight, there issued forth from the effulgent flame that quenched it a breath that made me attentive, and it said, 'Until you have again the sense of sight which you have consumed in me, it is well that you compensate it by discourse. Begin then, and say on what aim your soul is set; and be assured that your sight in you is confounded, not destroyed; for the lady who guides you through this divine region has in her look the power which the hand of Ananias had.'

And I said, 'At her good pleasure, soon or late, let succor come to the eyes which were the doors when she did enter with the fire wherewith I ever burn. The good which satisfies this Court is Alpha and Omega of all the scripture which Love reads to me, either low or loud.'

The same voice that had delivered me from my fear at the sudden dazzlement gave me concern to speak again; and it said, 'Assuredly you must sift with a finer sieve: you must tell who directed your bow to such a target.'

And I, 'By philosophic arguments, and by authority that descends from here, such love must needs imprint itself on me; for the good, inasmuch as it is good, kindles love in proportion as it is understood, and so much the more the more of good it contains in itself. Therefore, to that Essence wherein is such supremacy that whatsoever good be found outside of It is naught else save a beam of Its own radiance, more than to any other must the mind be moved, in love, of whoever discerns the truth on which this proof is founded. Such a truth he makes plain to my intelligence who demonstrates to me the first love of all the eternal substances. The voice of the veracious Author makes it plain where, speaking of Himself, He says to Moses, 'I will make you see all goodness.' You also set it forth to me in the beginning of your sublime proclamation, which more than any other heralding, declares below the mystery of this place on high.'

And I heard, 'On the ground of human reason and of the authorities concordant with it, the highest of all your loves looks to God; but tell me also if you feel other cords draw you toward Him, so that you declare with how many teeth this love grips you.'

The holy intention of the Eagle of Christ was not hidden, indeed it was plain to me whither he would direct my profession. Therefore I began again, 'All those things whose bite can make the heart turn to God have wrought together in my love; for the being of the world and my own being, the death that He sustained that I might live, and that which every believer hopes, as do I, with the living assurance of which I spoke, have drawn me from the sea of perverse love and placed me on the shore of right love. The leaves wherewith all the garden of the Eternal Gardener is enleaved I love in measure of the good borne unto them from Him.'

As soon as I was silent a most sweet song resounded through the heaven, and my lady sang with the rest, 'Holy, Holy, Holy!' And as sleep is broken by a piercing light when the visual spirit runs to meet the splendor that goes from tunic to tunic, and he who awakens shrinks from what he sees, so ignorant is his sudden awakening, until his judgment comes to his aid; thus Beatrice chased away every mote from my eyes with the radiance of her own, which shone more than a thousand miles; so that I then saw better than before; and as one amazed I asked concerning a fourth light which I saw with us. And my lady, 'Within those rays the first soul which the First Power ever created gazes with love upon its Maker.'

As the bough which bends its top at passing of the wind, and then uplifts itself by its own virtue which raises it, so did I, in amazement, while she was speaking, and then a desire to speak, wherewith I was burning, gave me assurance again, and I began, 'O fruit that were alone produced mature, O ancient father of whom every bride is daughter and daughter-in-law, devoutly as I can, I implore you that you speak to me: you see my wish, and that I may hear you sooner I do not tell it.'

Sometimes an animal that is covered so stirs that its impulse must needs be apparent, since what envelops it follows its movements: in like manner that first soul showed me, through its covering, how joyously it came to do me pleasure. Then it breathed forth, 'Without its being told to me by you, I discern your wish better than you whatever is most certain to you, for I see it in the truthful Mirror which makes of Itself a reflection of all else, while of It nothing makes itself the reflection. You wish to know how long it is since God placed me in the lofty garden wherein this lady prepared you for so long a stair; and how long it was a delight to my eyes; and the true cause of the great wrath; and the idiom which I used and shaped. Now know, my son, that the tasting of the tree was not in itself the cause of so long an exile, but solely the overpassing of the bound. In the place whence your lady dispatched Virgil, I longed for this assembly during four thousand three hundred and two revolutions of the sun; and while I was on earth I saw him return to all the lights of his path nine hundred and thirty times. The tongue which I spoke was all extinct before the people of Nimrod attempted their unaccomplishable work; for never was any product of reason durable forever, because of human liking, which alters, following the heavens. That man should speak is nature's doing, but whether thus or thus, nature then leaves you to follow your own pleasure. Before I descended to the anguish of Hell the Supreme Good from whom comes the joy that swathes me was named *I* on earth; and later He was called *El*: and that must needs be, for the usage of mortals is as a leaf on a branch, which goes away and another comes. On the mountain which rises highest from the sea I lived pure, then guilty, from the first hour to that which follows, when the sun changes quadrant, next upon the sixth.

CANTO XXVII

'GLORY BE to the Father, to the Son, and to the Holy Spirit!' all Paradise began, so that the sweet song held me rapt. What I saw seemed to me a smile of the universe, so that my rapture entered both by hearing and by sight. O joy! O ineffable gladness! O life entire of love and of peace! O wealth secure without longing!

Before my eyes the four torches stood enkindled, and that which had come first began to make itself more vivid, and in its aspect became as would Jupiter if he and Mars were birds and should exchange plumage. The Providence which there assigns turn and office had imposed silence on the blessed choir on every side, when I heard, 'If I change color, marvel not, for, as I speak, you shall see all these change color. He who on earth usurps my place, my place, my place, which in the sight of the Son of God is vacant, has made my burial-ground a sewer of blood and of stench, so that the Perverse One who fell from here above takes comfort there below.'

With that color which, by reason of the opposite sun, paints the cloud at evening and at morning, I then saw the whole heaven over-spread. And as a chaste lady who is sure of herself, and at another's fault, only hearing of it, becomes timid, so did Beatrice change her semblance; and such, I believe, was the eclipse in heaven when the Supreme Power suffered.

Then his words continued, in a voice so altered from itself that his looks were not more changed, 'The spouse of Christ was not nurtured on my blood and that of Linus and of Cletus, to be employed for gain of gold; but for gain of this happy life Sixtus and Pius and Calixtus and Urban shed their blood after much weeping. It was not our purpose that one part of the Christian people should sit on the right of our successors, and one part on the left;

nor that the keys which were committed to me should become the ensign on a banner for warfare on the baptized; nor that I should be made a figure on a seal to sold and lying privileges, whereat I often blush and flash. Rapacious wolves, in shepherd's garb, are seen from here above in all the pastures: O defense of God, wherefore dost thou yet lie still? Cahor-sines and Gascons make ready to drink our blood. O good beginning to what vile ending must you fall! But the high Providence, which with Scipio defended for Rome the glory of the world, will succor speedily, as I conceive. And you, my son, who, because of your mortal weight will again return below, open your mouth and do not hide what I hide not.'

Even as our air, when the horn of the heavenly Goat is touched by the sun, flakes down frozen vapors, so I saw the ether thus adorned, flaking upwards triumphal vapors which had made sojourn with us there. My sight was following their semblances, and followed, till the intermediate space became so great that it took from it the power of passing farther onward. Whereon my lade, who saw me freed from gazing upwards, said to me, 'Cast your sight down and see how far you have revolved.'

From the time when I had looked before, I saw that I had moved through the whole arc which the first climate makes from its middle to its end; so that, on the one hand, beyond Cadiz, I saw the mad track of Ulysses, and on the other nearly to the shore where Europa made herself a sweet burden; and more of the space of this little threshing-floor would have been disclosed to me, but the sun was proceeding beneath my feet and was a sign and more away.

My enamored mind, which ever pays court to my lady, was more than ever burning to bring back my eyes to her; and if nature or art ever made baits to take the eye so as to possess the mind, in human flesh or in its portraiture, all these together would seem as nothing beside the divine delight that glowed upon me when I turned to her smiling face. And the power which her look granted me drew me forth from the fair nest of Leda and thrust me into the swiftest of the heavens.

Its parts, most living and exalted, are so

uniform that I cannot tell which of them Beatrice chose as a place for me. But she, who saw my longing, began, smiling so glad that God seemed to rejoice in her countenance, 'The nature of the universe which holds the center quiet and moves all the rest around it, begins here as from its starting-point. And this heaven has no other *Where* than the divine mind, wherein is kindled the love that revolves it, and the virtue which it rains down. Light and love enclose it in a circle, as it does the others, and this engirdment He alone who girds it understands. Its motion is not determined by another's, but the others are measured by this, just as ten by its half and its fifth. And how time should have its roots in such a flower-pot, and in the others its leaves, may now be manifest to you.

'O greed, who do so plunge mortals in your depths that none has power to life his eyes from your waves! The will blossoms well in men, but the continual rain turns the sound plums into blighted fruit. Faith and innocence are found only in little children; then each flies away before the cheeks are covered. One, so long as he lisps, keeps the fasts, who afterward, when his tongue is free, devours any food through any month; and one, while he lisps, loves his mother and listens to her, who afterward, when his speech is full, longs to see her buried. Thus the white skin turns black at the first sight of the fair daughter of him that brings morning and leaves evening. That you marvel not at this, consider that on earth there is no one to govern, wherefore the human family goes thus astray. But before January be all unwintered, because of the hundredth part that is neglected below, these lofty circles shall so shine forth that the storm which has been so long awaited shall turn round the sterns to where the prows are, so that the fleet shall run straight; and good fruit shall follow on the flower.'

CANTO XXVIII

AFTER SHE who imparadises my mind had declared the truth counter to the present life of wretched mortals, as one who sees in a mirror the flame of a torch which is lighted behind him before he has it in sight or in thought, and turns round to see if the glass tells him the truth, and sees that it accords with it as a song with its measure, so my memory recalls that I did, gazing into the beautiful eyes wherewith Love made the cord to capture me. And when I turned and my own were met by what appears in that revolving sphere whenever one gazes intently on its circling, I saw a point which radiated a light so keen that the eye on which it blazes needs must close because of its great keenness; and whatever star seems smallest from here would seem a moon if placed beside it like a star with neighboring star.

Perhaps as near as a halo seems to girdle the light which paints it, when the vapor that bears it is most dense, at such distance around the point a circle of fire was whirling so rapidly that it would have surpassed that motion which most swiftly girds the universe; and this was girt around by another, and that by a third, and the third by a fourth, by a fifth the fourth, then by a sixth the fifth. Thereon the seventh followed, now spread so wide that the messenger of Juno entire would be too narrow to contain it. So the eighth and the ninth; and each was moving more slowly according as it was in number more distant from the unit. And that one had the clearest flame from which the pure spark was least distant, because, I believe, it partakes more of its truth.

My lady, who saw me eager and in great suspense, said, 'On that point the heavens and all nature are dependent. Look on that circle which is most conjoined to it, and know that its motion is so swift because of the burning love whereby it is spurred.'

And I to her, 'If the universe were disposed in the order which I see in those wheels, that which is set before me would have satisfied me. But in the world of sense the revolutions may be seen so much the more divine as they are more remote from the center. Wherefore if my desire is to attain to its end in this wondrous and angelic temple which has only love and light for its confine, needs must I further hear why the model and the copy go not in one fashion, for by myself I contemplate this in vain.'

'If your fingers are insufficient for such a knot, it is no wonder, so hard has it become by not being tried.' So said my lady, then she continued, 'Take that which I shall tell you, if you would be satisfied, and sharpen your wits about it. The material spheres are wide or narrow according to the more or less of virtue which is diffused through all their parts. Greater goodness must needs work greater weal; and the greater body, if it has its parts equally complete, contains the greater weal. Hence this sphere, which sweeps along with it all the rest of the universe, corresponds to the circle which loves most and knows most. Wherefore, if you draw your measure round the virtue, not the semblance, of the substances which appear to you in circles, you will see a wondrous correspondence of greater to more and of smaller to less, in each heaven with respect to its Intelligence.'

As the hemisphere of the air remains splendid and serene when Boreas blows from his milder cheek, whereby the obscuring mist is cleared and dissolved, so that the heaven smiles to us with the beauties of its every region, so I became after my lady had provided me with her clear answer, and like a star in heaven the truth was seen.

And when she had paused in her speech, not otherwise does molten iron throw out sparks than the circles sparkled. Each spark kept to its fiery ring, and they were so many that their number stretches to more thousands than the doubling of the chessboard. I heard Hosannah sung from choir to choir to the fixed point that holds them, and will forever hold them at the *Ubi* in which they have ever been. And she, who saw the questioning thoughts within my mind, said, 'The first circles have shown to you the Seraphim and the Cherubim. Thus swiftly they follow their bonds, in order to liken themselves to the point as most they can, and they can in proportion as they are exalted in vision. Those other loves who go round them are called Thrones of the divine aspect, because they terminated the first triad. And you should know that all have delight in the measure of the depth to which their sight penetrates the Truth in which every intellect finds rest; from which it may be seen that the state of blessedness is founded on the act of vision, not on that which loves, which follows after; and the merit, to which grace and good will give birth, is the measure of their vision; thus, from grade to grade the progression goes.

'The next triad that thus flowers in this eternal spring which nightly Aries does not despoil perpetually sings Hosannah with three melodies which sound in the three orders of bliss that form the triad. In this hierarchy are the next divinities, first Dominions, then Virtues; and the third are Powers. Then in the two penultimate dances, the Principalities and Archangels circle; the last is wholly of Angelic sports. These orders all gaze upward and prevail downward, so that toward God all are drawn, and all do draw. And Dionysius with such great desire set himself to contemplate these orders that he named and distinguished them, as I: but Gregory afterward differed from him, wherefore, as soon as he opened his eyes in this heaven, he smiled at himself. And if a mortal declared on earth so much of secret truth, I would not have you wonder, for he who saw it here on high disclosed it to him, with much else of the truth about these circles.'

CANTO XXIX

WHEN THE two children of Latona, covered by the Ram and by the Scales, make the horizon their belt at one same moment, as long as from the instant when the zenith holds them balanced till the one and the other, changing hemispheres, are unbalanced from that belt, for so long, her face illumined with a smile, was Beatrice silent, looking fixedly at the point, which had overcome me. Then she began, 'I tell, not ask, what you wish to hear, for I have seen it there where every *ubi* and every *quando* is centered. Not for gain of good unto Himself, which cannot be, but that His splendor might, in resplendence, say, '*Subsisto*' – in His eternity beyond time, beyond every other bound, as it pleased Him, the Eternal Love opened into new loves. Nor before, as if inert, did He lie, for neither before nor after did the moving of God upon these waters proceed. Form and matter, conjoined and simple, came into being which had no defect, as three arrows from a three-stringed bow; and as in glass, in amber, or in crystal, a ray shines so that there is no interval between its coming and its pervading all, so did the triform effect ray forth from its Lord into its being, all at once, without distinction of beginning. Therewith order was created and ordained for the substances; and those in whom pure act was produced were the summit of the universe. Pure potentiality held the lowest place; in the middle such a bond tied up potentiality with act that it is never unbound. Jerome wrote for you of the angels as being created a long stretch of ages before aught else of the universe was made; but the truth I tell is written on many a page of the scribes of the Holy Spirit, and you shall be aware of it if you look well; and also reason sees it somewhat, which would not admit that the movers could be so long without their perfection. Now you know where and when these Loves were created, and how; so that three flames of your desire are already quenched.

Then, sooner than one might count to twenty, a part of the Angels disturbed the substrate of your elements. The rest remained and with such great delight began this art which you behold that they never cease from circling. The origin of the fall was the accursed pride of him whom you have seen constrained by all the weights of the universe. Those whom you see here were modest to recognize their being as from the Goodness which had made them apt for intelligence so great: wherefore their vision was exalted with illuminating grace and with their merit, so that they have their will full and established. And I would not have you doubt, but be assured that to receive grace is meritorious, in proportion as the affection is open to it.

'By now, if you have taken in my words, you may contemplate much in regard to this consistory without more help. But since it is taught in your schools on earth that the angelic nature is such that it understands and remembers and wills, I will speak further, in order that you may see in purity the truth that down there is confounded by the equivocation in such like teaching. These substances, since first they were gladdened by the face of God, have never turned their eyes from It, wherefrom nothing is concealed; so that their sight is never intercepted by a new object, and therefore they have no need to remember by reason of interrupted concept. Thus down there men dream while awake, believing or not believing that they speak truth – but in the one case is the greater blame and shame. You mortals do not proceed along one same path in philosophizing, so much does the love of show and the thought of it carry you away; and even this is borne with less anger up here than when the Divine Scripture is set aside or when it is perverted. They think not there how much blood it costs to sow it in the world, nor how much he pleases who humbly keeps close to it. Each one strives for display and makes his own inventions, and these are treated of by the preachers, and the Gospel is silent. One says that at Christ's passion the moon turned back and interposed itself, so that the light of the sun did not reach below – and he lies, for the light itself hid itself, so that this eclipse took place for the Spaniards and the Indians, as well as for the Jews. Florence has not so many Lapos and Bindos as fables such as these that are shouted the year long from the pulpits on every side; so that the poor sheep, who know naught, return from the pasture fed with wind – and not seeing the harm does not excuse them. Christ did not say to his first company, "Go and preach idle stories to the world," but he gave to them the true foundation; and that alone sounded on their lips, so that to fight for kindling of the faith they made shield and lance of the Gospel. Now men go forth to preach with jests and with buffooneries, and so there be only a good laugh, the cowl puffs up and nothing more is asked. But such a bird nests in the hood's tail that if the people saw it, they would see what pardons they are trusting in; from which such folly has grown on earth that without proof of any testimony they would flock to every promise. On this the pig of St. Anthony fattens, and others also, who are far more pigs, paying with money that has no stamp of coinage.

'But since we have digressed enough, turn back your eyes now to the true path, so that the way be shortened with the time. This nature extends so exceedingly in number that never was there speech or mortal concept that might advance so far; and if you look at that which is revealed by Daniel, you will see that in his thousands no definite number is to be found. The Primal Light that irradiates them all is received by them in as many ways as are the splendors to which It joins Itself. Wherefore, since the affection follows upon the act of conceiving the sweetness of love glows variously in them, more and less. Behold now the height and breadth of the Eternal Goodness, since it has made itself so many mirrors wherein it is reflected, remaining itself One as before.'

CANTO XXX

THE SIXTH hour is glowing perhaps six thousand miles away, and this world already slopes its shadow almost to a level bed, when the midst of heaven deep above us begins to grow such that a star here and there is lost to sight at this depth; and as the brightest handmaid of the sun advances, the heaven then shuts off its lights one by one, till the fairest is gone; not otherwise the triumph that plays forever round the Point which overcame me, seeming enclosed by that which it encloses, was gradually extinguished to my sight, wherefore seeing nothing and love constrained me to return with my eyes to Beatrice. If what has been said of her so far as here were all included in a single praise, it would be too slight to serve this present turn. The beauty I beheld transcends measure not only beyond our reach, but I truly believe that He alone who made it can enjoy it all. At this pass I concede myself defeated more than ever comic or tragic poet was defeated by a point in his theme; for, as the sun does to the sight which trembles most, even so remembrance of the sweet smile shears my memory of its very self. From the first day when in this life I saw her face, until this sight, the continuing of my song has not been cut off, but now my pursuit must desist from following her beauty further in my verses, as at his utmost reach must every artist.

Such as I leave her to a greater heralding than that of my trumpet, which draws its arduous subject to a close, with the act and voice of a leader whose task is accomplished she began again, 'We have issued forth from the greatest body to the heaven which is pure light: light intellectual full of love, love of true good full of joy, joy that transcends every sweetness. Here you shall see the one and the other soldiery of Paradise, and the one in those aspects which you shall see at the last judgment.'

As a sudden flash of lightning which scatters the visual spirits so that it robs the eye of the sight of the clearest objects, so round about me there shone a vivid light and left me so swathed in the veil of its effulgence that nothing was visible to me.

'Ever does the love which quiets this heaven receive into itself with such like salutation, in order to prepare the candle for its flame.' No sooner had these brief words come within me than I comprehended that I was surmounting beyond my own power, and such new vision was kindled in me that there is no light so bright that my eyes could not have withstood it. And I saw a light in form of a river glowing tawny between two banks painted with marvelous spring. From out this river issued living sparks and dropped on every side into the blossoms, like rubies set in gold. Then, as if inebriated by the odors, they plunged again into the wondrous flood, and as one was entering another was issuing forth.

'The high desire which now inflames and urges you to have knowledge concerning that which you see pleases me the more the more it swells; but first you must needs drink of this water before so great a thirst in you be slaked.' So spoke the sun of my eyes to me, then added, 'The stream and the topazes which enter and issue, and the smiling of the grasses, are the shadowy prefaces of their truth; not that these things are defective in themselves, but on your side is the defect, in that you do not yet have vision so exalted.'

No infant, on waking far after its hour, so suddenly rushes with face toward the milk, as then did I, to make yet better mirrors of my eyes, stooping to the wave which flows there that we may be bettered in it. And even as the eaves of my eyelids drank of it, so it seemed to me out of its length to have become round. Then, as folk who have been under masks seem other than before, if they do off the semblances not their own wherein they were hid, so into greater

festival the flowers and the sparks did change before me that I saw both the courts of Heaven made manifest. O splendor of God whereby I saw the high triumph of the true kingdom, give to me power to tell how I beheld it!

A Light is thereabove which makes the Creator visible to every creature that has his peace only in beholding Him. It spreads so wide a circle that the circumference would be too large a girdle for the sun. Its whole expanse is made by a ray reflected from the summit of the Primum Mobile, which therefrom takes its life and potency; and as a hillside mirrors itself in water at its base, as if to look upon its own adornment when it is rich in grasses and in flowers, so above the light round and round about in more than a thousand tiers I saw all that of us have won return up there. And if the lowest rank encloses within itself so great a light, how vast is the spread of this rose in its outermost leaves! My sight lost not itself in the breadth and in the height, but took in all the extent and quality of that joy. There, near and far neither add nor take away, for where God governs without intermediary, the law of nature in no way prevails.

Into the yellow of the eternal Rose, which rises in ranks and expands and breathes forth odor of praise unto the Sun which makes perpetual spring, Beatrice drew me as one who is silent and wishes to speak, and she said, 'Behold how great the assembly of the white robes! See our city, how wide is its circuit! See our seats so filled that few souls are now wanted there!

'And in that great chair whereon you fix your eyes because of the crown that already is set above it, before you sup at these nuptials shall sit the soul, which on earth will be imperial, of the lofty Henry, who will come to set Italy straight before she is ready. The blind cupidity which bewitches you has made you like the little child who dies of hunger and drives away his nurse. And such a one will then be prefect in the divine forum who openly and secretly will not go with him along one same road. But not for long shall God then suffer him in the holy office; for he shall be thrust down where Simon Magus is for his deserts, and shall make him of Alagna go deeper still.'

Canto XXXI

IN FORM then of a pure white rose the saintly host was shown to me, which with His own blood Christ made His bride. But the other host — who, as it flies, sees and sings His glory who enamors it and the goodness which made it so great — like a swarm of bees which one moment enflower themselves, and the next return to where their work acquires savor — was descending into the great flower which is adorned with so many petals, and thence reascending to where its love abides forever. They had their faces all of living flame, and their wings of gold, and the rest so white that no snow reaches such a limit. When they descended into the flower, from rank to rank they proffered of the peace and the ardor which they had acquired as they fanned their sides. Nor did the interposing of so great a flying plenitude, between what was above and the flower, impede the vision or the splendor; for the divine light so penetrates through the universe, in measure of its worthiness, that naught can be an obstacle to it. This secure and joyful kingdom, thronged with ancient and with modern folk, had look and love all directed on one mark.

O threefold Light, which, in a single star sparkling on their sight, dost so satisfy them, look down upon our tempest here below!

If the Barbarians, coming from such region as is covered every day by Helice, wheeling with her son whom she delights in, when they beheld Rome and her mighty work, when Lateran rose above all mortal things, were wonder-struck, I, who to the divine from the human, to the eternal from time had come, and from Florence to a people just and sane, with what amazement must I have been full! Truly, what with it and with the joy, I was content to hear naught and to stand mute. And as a pilgrim who is refreshed within the temple of his vow as he looks around, and already hopes to tell again how it was, so, taking my way upwards through the living light, I led my eyes along the ranks, now up, now down, and now circling about. I saw faces all given to love, adorned by the light of Another, and by their own smile, and movements graced with every dignity.

My look had now taken in the general form of Paradise as a whole, and on no part as yet had my sight paused; and I turned with rekindled will to ask my lady about things as to which my mind was in suspense. One thing I purposed, and another answered me: I thought to see Beatrice, and I saw an elder, clad like the folk in glory. His eyes and cheeks were suffused with benign gladness, his mien kindly such as befits a tender father. And, 'Where is she?' I said at once; whereon he, 'To terminate your desire Beatrice urged me from my place; and if you look up to the circle which is third from the highest tier, you will see her again, in the throne her merits have allotted to her.

Without answering I lifted up my eyes and saw her where she made for herself a crown as she reflected the eternal rays. From the region which thunders most high no mortal eye is so far distant, were it plunged most deep within the sea, as there from Beatrice was my sight. But to me it made no difference, for her image came down to me unblurred by aught between.

'O lady, in whom my hope is strong, and who for my salvation did endure to leave in Hell your footprints, of all those things which I have seen I acknowledge the grace and the virtue to be from your power and your excellence. It is you who have drawn me from bondage into liberty by all those paths, by all those means by which you had the power so to do. Preserve in me your great munificence, so that my soul, which you have made whole, may be loosed from the body, pleasing unto you.' So did I pray; and she, so distant as she seemed, smiled and looked on me, then turned again to the eternal fountain.

And the holy elder said, 'In order that you may consummate your journey perfectly, whereto prayer and holy love dispatched me, fly with your eyes throughout this garden; for gazing on it will better prepare your sight to mount through the divine ray. And the Queen of Heaven, for whom I am all afire with love, will grant us every grace, since I am her faithful Bernard.'

As is he who comes perchance from Croatia to look on our Veronica, and whose old hunger is not sated, but says in thought so long as it is shown, 'My Lord Jesus Christ, true God, was

then your semblance like to this?' such was I, gazing on the living charity of him who, in this world, in contemplation tasted of that peace.

'Son of grace, this joyous being,' he began, 'will not be known to you if you hold your eyes down here at the base; but look upon the circles, even to the most remote, until you see upon her seat the Queen to whom this realm is subject and devoted.'

I lifted up my eyes; and as at morning the eastern parts of the horizon outshine that where the sun declines, so, as if going with my eyes from valley to mountain-top, I saw a part on the extreme verge surpass with its light all the rest of the rim. And as the point where we await the pole that Phaethon misguided is most aglow, and on this side and on that the light diminishes, so was that pacific oriflamme quickened in the middle, on either side in equal measure tempering its flame. And at the midpoint, with outstretched wings, I saw more than a thousand Angels making festival, each one distinct in effulgence and in ministry. I saw there, smiling to their sports and to their songs, a beauty which was gladness in the eyes of all the other saints. And had I equal wealth in speech as in conception, yet would I not dare to attempt the least of her delightfulness.

Bernard, when he saw my eyes fixed and intent on the object of his own burning glow, turned his own with such affection to her, that he made mine more ardent in their gazing.

CANTO XXXII

WITH HIS love fixed on his Delight, that contemplator freely assumed the office of a teacher, and began these holy words, 'The wound which Mary closed and anointed, that one who is so beautiful at her feet is she who opened it and pierced it. Below her, in the order which the third seats make, sits Rachel with Beatrice, as you see. Sarah, Rebecca, Judith, and she who was great-grandmother of the singer who, through sorrow for his sin, cried 'Miserere mei,' you may see, thus from rank to rank in gradation downward, as with the name of each I go downward through the rose from petal to petal. And from the seventh row

downwards, even as down to it, Hebrew women follow in succession, dividing all the tresses of the flower; because, according to the look which their faith turned to Christ, these are the wall by which the sacred stairway is divided. On this side, wherein the flower is mature in all its petals, are seated those who believed in Christ yet to come. On the other side, where the half-circles are broken by vacant places, sit those who turned their faces toward Christ already come. And as on this side the glorious seat of the Lady of Heaven, and the other seats below it, make so great a partition, thus, opposite, does the seat of the great John who, ever holy, endured the desert and martyrdom, and then Hell for two years; and beneath him, Francis and Benedict and Augustine and others were allotted thus to divide, as far down as here, from circle to circle. Now behold the depth of the divine foresight, for one and the other aspect of the faith shall fill this garden equally. And know that, downward from the row which cleaves midway the two dividing lines, they are seated for no merit of their own, but for that of others, under certain conditions; for all these are spirits absolved before they had true power of choice. Well can you perceive it by their faces and by their childish voices, if you look well upon them and if you listen to them.

'Now you are perplexed, and in perplexity are silent; but I will loose the hard knot wherein your subtle thoughts are binding you. Within the amplitude of this realm a casual point can have no place, any more than can sorrow, or thirst, or hunger; for whatever you see is established by eternal law, so that the correspondence is exact between the ring and finger. And therefore this company, hastened to true life, is not *sine causa* more or less excellent here among themselves. The King, through whom this realm reposes in such great love and in such great delight that no will dares for more, creating all the minds in His glad sight, at His own pleasure endows with grace diversely — and here let the fact suffice. And this is clearly and expressly noted for you in Holy Scripture in those twins whose anger was stirred within their mother's womb. Therefore, according to the color of the locks, of such grace needs must the lofty light crown them according to their worth. Wherefore, without merit of their own works, they are placed in different ranks, differing only in the primal keenness of vision. In the early ages, their parents' faith alone, with their own innocence, sufficed for their salvation; after those first ages were complete, it was needful for males, through circumcision, to acquire power for their innocent wings; but after the time of grace had come, without perfect baptism in Christ such innocence was held there below.

'Look now upon the face which most resembles Christ, for only its brightness can prepare you to see Christ.'

I saw such gladness rain down upon her, borne in the holy minds created to fly through that height, that all I had seen before had not held me in suspense of such great marveling, nor showed me such likeness to God. And that Love which first descended there, singing '*Ave Maria, gratia plena*,' now spread his wings before her. On all sides the blessed Court responded to the divine song, so that every face became the brighter therefor.

'O holy father, who for my sake endure to be here below, leaving the sweet place in which by eternal lot you have your seat, who is that angel who with such joy looks into the eyes of our Queen, so enamored that he seems afire?' Thus did I again recur to the teaching of him who drew beauty from Mary, as the morning star from the sun.

And he to me, 'Confidence and grace, as much as there can be in angel and in soul, are all in him, and we would have it so, for it is he who bore the palm down to Mary, when the Son of God willed to load Himself with the burden of our flesh.

'But come now with your eyes, as I proceed in speaking, and note the great patricians of this most just and pious empire. Those two who sit there above, most happy for being nearest to the Empress, are, as it were, two roots of this rose: he who is beside her upon the left is that Father because of whose audacious tasting the human race tastes such bitterness. On the right you see that ancient Father of Holy Church to whom Christ entrusted the keys of this beauteous flower. And he who saw, before he died, all the grievous times of the fair Bride who was won with the spear and the nails sits at his side; and beside the other rests that leader, under whom the thankless, fickle, and stubborn people lived on manna. Opposite Peter you see Anna sitting, so content to gaze upon her daughter that she moves not her eyes as she sings Hosannah. And opposite the greatest father of a family sits Lucy, who moved your lady when you were bending your brows downward to your ruin.

'But because the time flies that brings sleep upon you, we will stop here, like a good tailor that cuts the garment according to his cloth, and we will turn our eyes to the Primal Love, so that, gazing toward Him, you may penetrate, as far as that can be, into His effulgence. But lest, perchance, you fall back, moving your wings and thinking to advance, grace must be obtained by prayer, grace from her who has power to aid you; and do you follow me with your affection so that your heart depart not from my words.'

And he began this holy prayer:

CANTO XXXIII

'VIRGIN MOTHER, daughter of thy Son, humble and exalted more than any creature, fixed goal of the eternal counsel, thou art she who didst so enoble human nature that its Maker did not disdain to become its creature. In thy womb was rekindled the Love under whose warmth this flower in the eternal peace has thus unfolded. Here thou art for us the noonday torch of charity, and below among mortals thou art the living fount of hope. Lady, thou art so great and so availest, that whoso would have grace and has not recourse to thee, his desire seeks to fly without wings. Thy loving-kindness not only succors him who asks, but oftentimes freely foreruns the asking. In thee is mercy, in thee pity, in thee munificence, in thee is found whatever of goodness is in any creature. Now this man, who from the lowest pit of the universe even to here has seen one by one the spiritual lives, implores thee of thy grace for power such that he may be able with his eyes to rise still higher toward the last salvation. And I, who never for my own vision burned more than I do for his, proffer to thee all my prayers, and pray that they be not scant, that with thy prayers thou wouldst dispel for him every cloud of his mortality, so that the Supreme Pleasure may be disclosed to him. Further I pray thee, Queen, who canst do whatsoever thou wilt, that thou preserve sound for him his affections, after so great a vision. Let thy protection vanquish human impulses. Behold Beatrice, with how many saints, for my prayers clasping their hands to thee.'

The eyes beloved and reverenced by God, fixed upon him who prayed, showed us how greatly devout prayers do please her; then they were turned to the Eternal Light, wherein we may not believe that any creature's eye finds its way so clear.

And I, who was drawing near to the end of all desires, raised to its utmost, even as I ought, the ardor of my longing. Bernard was signing to me with a smile to look upward, but I was already of myself such as he wished; for my sight, becoming pure, was entering more and more through the beam of the lofty Light which in Itself is true.

Thenceforward my vision was greater than speech can show, which fails at such a sight, and at such excess memory fails. As is he who dreaming sees, and after the dream the passion remains imprinted and the rest returns not to the mind; such am I, for my vision almost wholly fades away, yet does the sweetness that was born of it still drop within my heart. Thus is the snow unsealed by the sun; thus in the wind, on the light leaves, the Sibyl's oracle was lost.

O Light Supreme that art so far uplifted above mortal conceiving, relend to my mind a little of what Thou didst appear, and give my tongue such power that it may leave only a single spark of Thy glory for the folk to come; for, by returning somewhat to my memory and by sounding a little in these lines, more of Thy victory shall be conceived.

I believe that, because of the keenness of the living ray, which I endured, I should have been lost if my eyes had been turned from it. I remember that on this account I was the bolder to sustain it, until I united my gaze with the Infinite Goodness.

O abounding grace whereby I presumed to fix my look through the Eternal Light so far that all my sight was spent therein.

In its depth I saw ingathered, bound by love in one single volume, that which is dispersed in leaves throughout the universe: substances and accidents and their relations, as though fused together in such a way that what I tell is but a simple light. The universal form of this knot I believe that I saw, because, in telling this, I feel my joy increase.

A single moment makes for me greater oblivion than five and twenty centuries have wrought upon the enterprise that made Neptune wonder at the shadow of the Argo. Thus my mind, all rapt, was gazing, fixed, motionless and intent, ever enkindled by its gazing. In that Light one becomes such that it is impossible he should ever consent to turn himself from it for other sight; for the good, which is the object of the will, is all gathered in it, and outside of it that is defective which is perfect there.

Now will my speech fall more short even in respect to that which I remember, than that of an infant who still bathes his tongue at the breast. Not because more than one simple semblance was in the Living Light wherein I was gazing, which ever is such as it was before; but through my sight, which was growing strong in me as I looked, one sole appearance, even as I changed, was altering itself to me.

Within the profound and shining subsistence of the lofty Light appeared to me three circles of three colors and one magnitude; and one seemed reflected by the other, as rainbow by rainbow, and the third seemed fire breathed forth equally from the one and the other.

O how scant is speech, and how feeble to my conception! and this, to what I saw, is such that it is not enough to call it little.

O Light Eternal, who alone abidest in Thyself, alone knowest Thyself, and, known to Theyself and knowing, lovest and smilest on Thyself!

That circling which, thus begotten, appeared in Thee as reflected light, when my eyes had dwelt on it for a time, seemed to me depicted with our image within itself and in its own color, wherefore my sight was entirely set upon it.

As is the geometer who wholly applies himself to measure the circle, and finds not, in pondering, the principle of which he is in need, such was I at that new sight. I wished to see how the image conformed to the circle and how it has its place therein; but my own wings were not sufficient for that, save that my mind was smitten by a flash wherein its wish came to it. Here power failed the lofty phantasy; but already my desire and my will were revolved, like a wheel that is evenly moved, by the Love which moves the sun and the other stars.